MASKS
THE ART OF EXPRESSION

EDITED BY JOHN MACK

MASKS

THE ART OF EXPRESSION

Published for The Trustees of

The British Museum by

BRITISH MUSEUM  PRESS

First published 1994
First published in paperback 1996
Reprinted 1998

A catalogue record for this book is available
from the British Library

ISBN 0 7141 2530 X

Designed by Harry Green

Typeset by Rowland Phototypesetting Ltd
Bury St Edmunds, Suffolk

Printed and bound in Singapore by Imago

Front jacket: Japanese No mask of Hannya,
a jealous and revengeful demon who was
once a beautiful woman. See fig. 86.
Black jacket: (top left): Cast gold mask from
Colombia. See fig. 41. (top right): Wood
mask from the North West coast of America.
See fig. 70. (lower left): Inlaid bronze mask,
Graeco-Roman. See fig. 106. (lower right):
Malanggan mask from Papua New Guinea.
See fig. 30.

Half title: Egyptian mummy mask.
See fig. 119.
Frontispiece: Alder mask from the
North West coast of America. See
fig. 69.
This spread: Hellenistic marble relief
of a dramatic mask. See fig. 112.

CONTENTS

PREFACE

This is a book about masks and masquerade, about what masks look like (and why) and about the circumstances of their use. It is also, to an extent, about broader cultural patterns, concepts of the body and the social or personal transformations implied in concealing or changing appearance. One assumption it makes is that such a subject will be familiar to most readers as an aspect of direct experience. There must be very few of us who have not at some point put on a mask or some equivalent device; still fewer who have not witnessed the surprise of someone else's appearance altered in masquerade.

Masking is a universal phenomenon, or virtually so. To reflect this in a single volume is, of course, impossible. There are inevitable geographical and cultural gaps, even given that some of the authors have been asked to take in the sweep and variety of masking practice on a continent-wide basis. Some of the unavoidable omissions in the general chapters are the subject of discussion and description in the introductory chapter, and the Bibliography seeks to give a broader range of reference to the world-wide distribution of masking practice.

It is also an indication of the comprehensive cultural basis of masquerade that the resources, both in terms of expertise and collections, of an institution with singular claim to universal coverage – the British Museum – have been extensively mined in the production of the book. The authors include social anthropologists, art historians, Classicists and Egyptologists. A number of separate Departments within the Museum have contributed, and the authors, with just one exception, are past or present members of the Museum's curatorial staff. In addition to those Departments who have supported the book, I should like to thank the British Museum's Photographic Service, who are responsible for most of the illustrations and, at British Museum Press, Rachel Rogers for getting the project off the ground and Carolyn Jones who has worked tirelessly to co-ordinate all our efforts.

JOHN MACK
Keeper of Ethnography

Mourner's dress, seen by Captain Cook on
his first voyage. Engraved by W. Woollett
from a drawing by W. Hodges. See fig. 36.

1. Japanese Nō mask of *Shikami*, a demon who appears in *Kiri Nō* plays such as *Rashōmon* and *Momijigari*. This is a male demon, and although there are similarities to the *Hannya* mask (see fig. 96), the form derives from the earlier *Kishin* mask. The actor's performance is accentuated by a rich costume and the use of a large red wig. The interior of the mask is inscribed '*Yodoishi Mitsunori*'. H. 21.5cm.

INTRODUCTION
ABOUT FACE

At first sight the topic of masks seems alluringly simple and self-contained. After all, we appear to be dealing with a single type of object. All masks are articulated by human agents. As a result masks are generally of predictable dimensions, and they often portray a face or head, usually human. Where the more diffuse subject of 'art' is notoriously difficult to define and discuss cross-culturally, 'masks' appears – superficially at least – to be a rather better-founded category.

Furthermore the use of masks, or of some closely related article such as the veil, is almost universal. As the various chapters here demonstrate, masks are known from cultures ranging from antiquity to the present, and from the South American Andes to the Far East. Masks are not merely something exotic which the Third World has and exploits while everyone else does not; nor, in Europe and America, are they only the faded remnant of some passing Arcadian tradition. A visiting Japanese anthropologist might examine the circumstances of the appearance of the Green Man in rural English festivals; yet contemporary Japanese Buddhism, quite apart from traditional theatre, provides a host of occasions for the display of masks. Equally, a children's party anywhere in Europe, America or indeed Japan, might provide a host of examples of masking using commercially-

2. African wood mask from Makuta near Tumba, Zaire. The context in which this large helmet mask, acquired in 1902, was used remains unrecorded. However, as with many masking traditions in Central Africa, a link to male initiation procedures (or funerary rites performed by the society of initiates on behalf of the community) is likely. H. 70cm.

produced masks impersonating a range of well-known characters and caricatures from public figures to popular heroes.

One of the more spontaneous sideshows occurring in London before the marriage of Prince Charles and Lady Diana, was the appearance of a cycling figure in full evening dress wearing a manufactured mask comically modelled on the well-known features of the groom. Riding down the Mall, the masker entertained the citizens gathering for the forthcoming spectacle – adding to the humour of the portrayal with appropriate royal waves. At the other end of the social scale a masked figure who is also a celebrated wrestler, Superbarrio (Superman), popularly appears in the poorer parts of Mexico City to drive away bailiffs arriving to evict tenants. In various forms masks are the stock-in-trade of as ill-assorted a group as participants in ritual, healers, theatrical and carnival performers, wrestlers, ball guests, executioners and their victims, burglars and terrorists, the Ku-Klux-Klan, welders and surgeons, ice-hockey players and fencers.

Masks are so familiar that on occasion it is assumed that objects from the past with quite pragmatic purposes were part of the elaborate artifice of masquerade. At the time of writing, for instance, one of the photographs appearing in the British Press is of a masker at a local fair wearing a mask with a large hooked nose. In fact, the mask is of a type worn by those who went out in medieval towns at the time of the Black Death to collect up the bodies of the unfortunate victims. The dominant visual feature, the exaggerated nose, was not developed the more completely to conceal the masker; stuffed full of sweet-smelling herbs, it acted rather to conceal the stench of death and was intended to prevent the spread of contagion. Recycled to cohere with contemporary expectation however, it is part of the fun and spectacle of medieval pageant. It is unquestioningly miscon-strued, but in a way that suggests that masks conform to a common and accessible system.

Equally, masks may still seem meaningful when abstracted from their appropriate cultural setting. There are many contexts in which they are presented as, in some way, emblematic. Tourist arts abound in mask styles which often bear little or no relation to the culture history they are supposed to sum up for the passing visitor: souvenirs of cultural forms which fre-quently never existed. Indeed in some places, masks are created for sale when masquerade was not in fact a part of local cultural patterns at all. The Maasai of Kenya and Tanzania are frequently represented in masks sold throughout East Africa, the distinctive pig-tailed hairstyle of the *moran*, the warrior grade, clearly portrayed. Yet the Maasai have virtually no tra-ditions of figurative carving, even less of portraiture and masking. In fact the masks are produced principally by the Akamba, the entrepreneurs of East African commercial carving. The author has also on one occasion bought a skilfully executed mask in the Shira-Punu style from Gabon.

3. A rare wood mask from the Solomon Islands, probably Bougainville, from the collection made by Charles Morris Woodford, a naturalist who travelled in the Solomons in the late 1880s. H. 41cm.

The mask, however, came from a market on the Indian Ocean island of Madagascar where it had been copied from a black and white illustration in a book. It was a uniform colour and not polychrome like the original; it was also pocket-sized, the concept of masks and masquerades not being a part of the island's culture and the carver never having seen a mask in use.

Masks are also a suitable subject to be represented in stamps. A casual check through a child's growing stamp collection shows examples from China, Mongolia and Angola. Similarly, folk troupes are frequently called on to express national identity through masked performance. In 1974 Pende masked dancers from Zaire performed in Germany in celebration of the national football team winning through to soccer's World Cup finals. The fact that their traditional role is to appear during male circumcision ceremonies, where they are regarded as something other than entertainers, was conveniently side-stepped.

Masking terminologies

Despite these assumptions about the universality of masks and their meanings, one indication that all is not as simple as it seems is the fact that the word 'mask' does not translate straightforwardly into many of the languages spoken by those who, none the less, have what we would like to think of as masking traditions. The emphasis of the term in English is on the act of concealment. 'Unmasking' is something that happens to spies and those with guilty secrets. Masking, masquerade, is disguise – and by extension perhaps even deception or pretence. The reference is to the altered appearance of the masker rather than to the status of the portrayal. Yet, as the examples of burglars and terrorists suggest, the wearing of a mask, while it may act to drain the masker of personal identity, is not inert even where it is intended only as concealment. Of itself a stocking mask asserts no other identity, yet the altered appearance of the wearer achieves menace whether or not the viewer feels personally threatened. In more playful context the staring, immobile masked face of even a close friend in party costume has a startling effect. The term 'mask' implicitly acknowledges human agency, that which is masked or concealed; but the resulting masquerade has a presence even if everyone is well aware that masking is, after all, only someone dressing up.

There are many societies in which the knowledge that someone is articulating the mask from within is officially denied. More precisely it may be denied to most people, that is, to those not in on the secret. As with the traditions surrounding the figure of Father Christmas in the Western World, the reality of the mechanics of masquerade may in practice gradually seep through to those who are not informed. Even so, in such situations masking is not subsequently presented as pretence. The whole emphasis

is less on what is concealed than on what is created. Indeed, even this may be an inadequate explanation in many cases, for often the origins of the entity presented in masquerade performance are elaborated in myth or oral tradition and not discussed as individual creation. In many parts of Central Africa, for instance, a generic term *makishi* or *nkisi* refers to a range of masks and to the performance of which masking is a part. These are normally spectacles that take place in the context of male circumcision ceremonies. But makishi are also said to be the dead in a resurrected form. The term is often translated as 'ancestral spirit'; one recorded technique of bringing such spirits to life is to break an egg over a tomb, rub it with palm oil, and utter a number of secret formulae known only to initiated men. In addition the word is used more broadly to refer to amulets, charms and related magical devices. This further set of associations indicates that makishi is a crucial term for the description of a whole range of primary animating forces. Our term 'mask' by contrast, carries only inanimate associations.

In Sri Lanka the situation is different and no less complex. There are two basic cycles of masked performance which occurred until recently in many parts of the island – these are Kolam and Sanni. Kolam is essentially a form of mythic drama or popular theatre in which the characters performing are masked; Sanni, on the other hand, is associated with rituals of healing, and specifically with the driving out of demons. According to Goonatilleka, the term Kolam can actually be adequately translated as 'mask' with the implication that the major emphasis is on the act of disguise which the masquerade effects. Elsewhere we learn that the origins of Kolam masked performance can be traced in myth to Vesamuni, the god of good fortune, who originally made Kolam masks to allay the sufferings of a Sinhalese Queen. Loviconi informs us that *vesa* means 'disguise' and *muhuna* 'face', hence 'false face' or 'mask'.

Yet, although there is an overlap between the two types of masked performance through their common association with curative ritual, in practice the terminology and the context of use separates them. Sanni translates as 'illness'. It is less a pageant than an attempt to exorcise evil spirits by representing in the presence of the patient and relatives the character of the illness brought about by particular demons. Interestingly, it is the mask cycle which has moved further from its original ritual functions in the direction of popular theatre that has carried with it references to the mask as 'false face'. Sanni simply is an embodiment of the illness – the mechanics of impersonation are not relevant. Indeed, masking is the final stage of a ritual which includes dancers entering temporary states of trance in which they themselves shake and become possessed by demons. Here the different cycles of masking, to the extent that they are related at all, seem to approach the issue of demonic possession from quite different

4. Mask from Satawan, Mortlock Islands, Federated States of Micronesia. Carved from breadfruit wood, with characteristic restrained painted decoration in white and black. H. 67cm.

directions. As Kapferer argues, comic masking points to a world outside itself and as such, contrasts with the all-engulfing process of possession.

Another habit of the English language that belies our expectations of general masking practice is that we tend to distinguish the mask from anything else that might be associated with it. We talk of the mask and separately, of the masquerade costume. A term like makishi, however, refers at once to the mask, the accompanying clothing and accoutrements, the character of the representation, and much else besides. Indeed the principal reference is to the masking spectacle itself and to a whole body of cultural knowledge about its implications, not to the mask as a single and separable object. This is inevitable where the mask is an element in a style of performance rich in symbolism and occurring at critical times in the lives of individuals and of society.

A main emphasis of this book is on the mask as artefact. However it must, inevitably, also concentrate on the cultural institution of masquerade or the event of masking. For in the end it is not the fact that the mask is an identifiable type of object which is common, but the fact that masking is a continuing and commonly-employed technique, a technique of transformation. We will also have to deal with the fact that in many instances the issue is not so clear cut. The transformation can be incomplete and the tension or interplay between what masquerade reveals and what it conceals is exactly what makes it intriguing – the mixture of the familiar and the strange.

Masks and transformations

There are a number of contexts documented in the chapters that follow, where the mask appears as an individual object, a separable icon. Yet the death mask of Classical cultures, a kind of static portrait with a viable existence outside any context of use, is the exception and not the rule. Where the effect of most acts of masquerade is to alter the appearance of the masker, the death mask seeks to freeze it. As the body deteriorates, the mask remains as a record of appearance, rather as a photograph survives more or less intact whilst over time the physical appearance of the subject portrayed alters.

A nice instance of this approximation to reality concerns the exhumation of the remains of J.S. Bach. Bach had died in 1750 and been interred at a certain spot in the Church of St John in Leipzig. When alterations were made to the Church in 1894, scholars attempted to identify Bach's coffin among a number found in the approximate place of his original burial. The sculptor Karl Seffner was brought in and from the skull, modelled the features of the deceased in the form of a retrospective death mask, rather as in parts of the Pacific human skulls are overmodelled to create a 'portrait' of the deceased. The result proved remarkably close to known painted portraits of Bach from the first half of the eighteenth century, and confirmed other evidence relating to the height of the deceased and to details of the coffin itself which already suggested the identity of the deceased. The remains were transferred to a permanent resting place beneath the altar of the Church.

All this contrasts with the use of masks in masquerade. Here the masker is transformed by the mask and costume. Yet the transformation is only temporary. After the performance the masker returns again to his (or occasionally her) original condition. Most masking is itself an act of transformation.

This apparent truism has wide implications. What, for instance, is the nature of the transformation effected in such cases? There can be no single answer to the question, for the simple reason that masquerade does two things: on the one hand it hides the masker, and on the other it introduces a new element, the masquerade and what that reveals. Negotiating the exact line between concealment and revelation in any given situation is one potent source of the variability of masking traditions. Furthermore every observer, in a sense, negotiates the line for themselves. It is not that each masquerade has a set purpose or symbolic content which is commonly understood. Knowledge of masking is not equally distributed among all members of a culture. An extended discussion of one introductory example makes this and a series of related points.

In Africa one of the richest masking traditions is that of the Chokwe, a people centred in northern Angola who have spread into Zaire and into parts of Zambia. The Chokwe have also been very influential outside their own immediate communities. Thus the Wiko, Chokwe migrants who have penetrated into Zambia, have introduced Chokwe-related masking traditions beyond the homelands in Angola, while the neighbouring Lunda have also adopted Chokwe styles. The Chokwe display masks principally in the course of circumcision rites and the masked figure is one of the leading subjects of Chokwe sculpture. The initiands are all boys usually between the ages of thirteen and fifteen and preferably chosen from among those who have already achieved puberty.

The circumcision process begins many months before the event of circumcision actually takes place. Potential candidates are reminded by the men of the village that they remain for the moment *idima*, that is uncircumcised or impure. Idima, they are told, are filth and unless circumcised will be unable to have relations with women or to father children. After an extended period, during which they undergo regular bouts of such taunts, the day eventually arrives when the circumcision itself is to take place. The idima are led off on a final tour of the village. Their ultimate destination is an enclosure some distance away where the operation will take place known as the 'place of dying'. They are escorted there for the first time by a masked

5. Stone mask, Teotihuacan, Mexico, AD 300–650. Highly stylised masks such as this may have been influenced by the Mezcala style from northeast Guerrero where a strong Teotihuacan presence has been detected. H. 22cm.

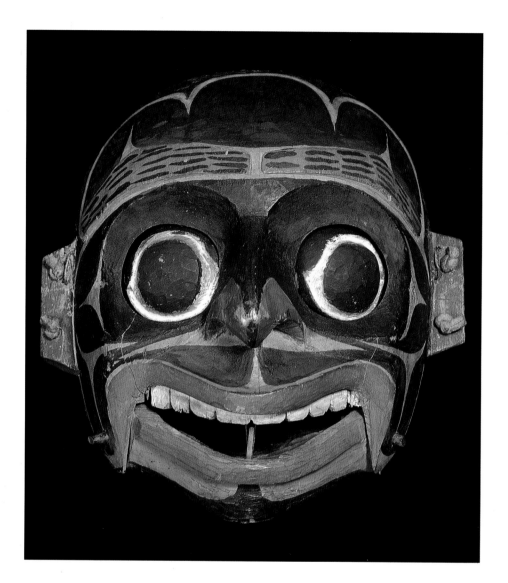

6. North American wood mask, probably representing a creature or spirit associated with a specific family tradition in the Winter Ceremonial. Collected, before 1868, at Fort Rupert, the Hudson's Bay Company post at the northern end of Vancouver island, where the Kwakwaka'wakw met and traded with other peoples from further north. H. 20cm.

figure. At this stage, to initiates as well as to women and children, the masker is a resurrected corpse.

Once at the circumcision ground the operation is quickly and accurately performed and considerable pride is taken in the ability to complete the surgery swiftly and competently – a lighted coal is sometimes thrown in the air and the act of circumcision finished before it hits the ground. The initiates then retire to the seclusion of the circumcision lodge while their wounds heal and they undergo the moral and practical instruction which permits their entry into the class of the circumcised. In the past this process lasted for as long as a year.

In practice most of the secrets of initiation amount to very little in substantive terms. One important piece of knowledge that is imparted, however, is the secret of masquerade: the esoteric information that masking is only, in the most basic terms, men transforming themselves into spirits. As they enter the seclusion lodge they are made one by one to remove the

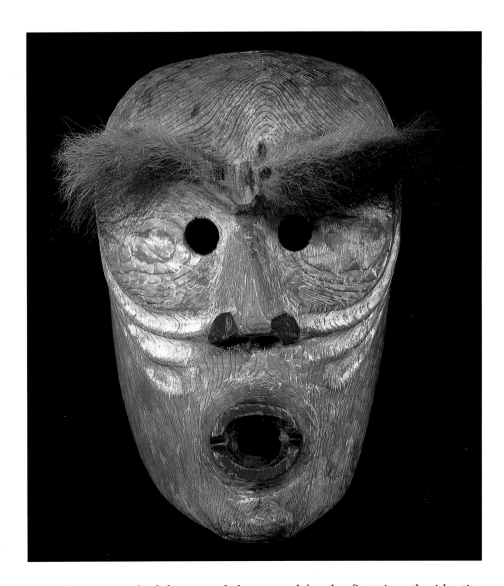

7. North American mask, Makah, Washington State, representing Bookwus, Wild Man of the Woods. Twentieth century. H. 23cm.

mask from a masked figure and thus reveal for the first time the identity of the masker. The initiates must swear an oath never to reveal to the uninitiated this or any other aspect of their instruction. This aura of secrecy is scrupulously maintained throughout the period of seclusion. When the initiates leave their camp to hunt or wash in a river they must always sing to warn of their coming so they may pass unseen by the uninitiated. On such outings their movements are carefully patrolled by a masked figure.

When the period of seclusion is at an end the candidates return to the village to show off newly-acquired skills at dancing. They move easily and gracefully despite their heavy fibre costume. At this stage if any of the initiates have died at the camp – or (in the parlance of rites of passage) failed to be reborn – a masked figure approaches the deceased's mother and gives her a piece of blackened calabash. Until that moment her son's death has been kept secret from her.

8. Japanese Nō mask of a *Shōjō*, a mythical sprite-like creature who lives in the water and who loves to drink *sake* when on land. In the play *Midare*, a merchant dreams of going to market to sell his *sake*. A stranger arrives and drinks a huge amount without getting drunk. The merchant discovers that the stranger is in fact a Shōjō who rewards him for his generosity with a flagon of *sake* which never runs dry. The Shōjō performs a lively dance which is enhanced by the use of a bright red wig and costume which emphasises the red mask, the colours symbolising drunkenness. The play shows the rewards that are available for those who do good deeds. The mask is inscribed 'Shōjō in the style of Himi of Etchu province'. H. 20.9cm.

The following morning at dawn the initiates go unobserved to a little-used river and burn all their initiation costumes in a hole. Then they wash and return naked to the village swearing on the way their oaths of secrecy. At the village, having left childhood and initiation behind, each initiate announces a new name by which he will henceforth be known and goes to the dancing ground where he dances with the once fearful maskers.

A common critique of masquerade in Africa and elsewhere is that it is only a trick by men to frighten women and children. Clearly in the Chokwe case the nature and impact of the transformation achieved by the masker depends very much on who you happen to be. For the circumcision candidate and uninitiated members of the family the appearance of the maskers to lead them off to 'the place of dying' is, given the unknown horrors that may be to come, a source of deep foreboding; yet to those who have already been through the circumcision process and who know its secrets, the fears must seem misplaced. The masker who carries a blackened calabash to the mother of a dead initiate is the source of the most contrary of emotions, distress to those who receive the calabash, relief to those who do not. And in the final events when the maskers dance with the successful initiates, they are liable to be upstaged by their supporting cast. The events now complete, the maskers on the point of departure, gifts are showered on the performers of the display. These are intended for the boys, not the maskers.

An important point the Chokwe example makes is the association of masking with other kinds of transformational event. It is very common for some form of masking to be associated with rites of passage or other ritual marking change. As this and successive chapters document, the events which are the occasion for masking are numerous. It can be found as part of the ceremonies of birth and death, and especially with the intervening steps of developing maturity, with initiation into adulthood and, where it is practised, circumcision. It occurs in the context of changes of status generally, whether it be promotion to some higher grade within a limited social grouping or even, on occasion, in association with such acts as accession to kingship. Masks are also a part of healing and other more personal ritual, where good health or good fortune becomes illness or bad luck. In some places masks are part of the judicial process. Indeed there is often very considerable overlap between these various events. Where there are masking societies, that is, groups within a given culture who organise and control masquerade, they may perform at any or all such occasions.

Masking can also mark annual and seasonal changes. In agriculturally-based communities the intervention of masks may help ensure that the crops grow well and they may be involved in ritual attending a successful harvest. The religious calendar provides another cycle of annual events

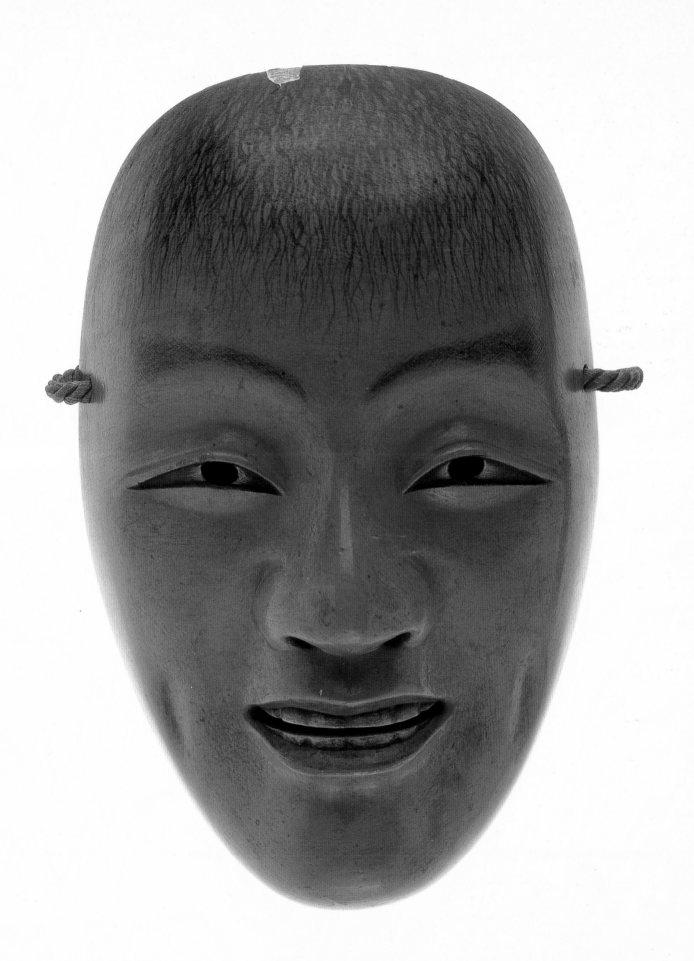

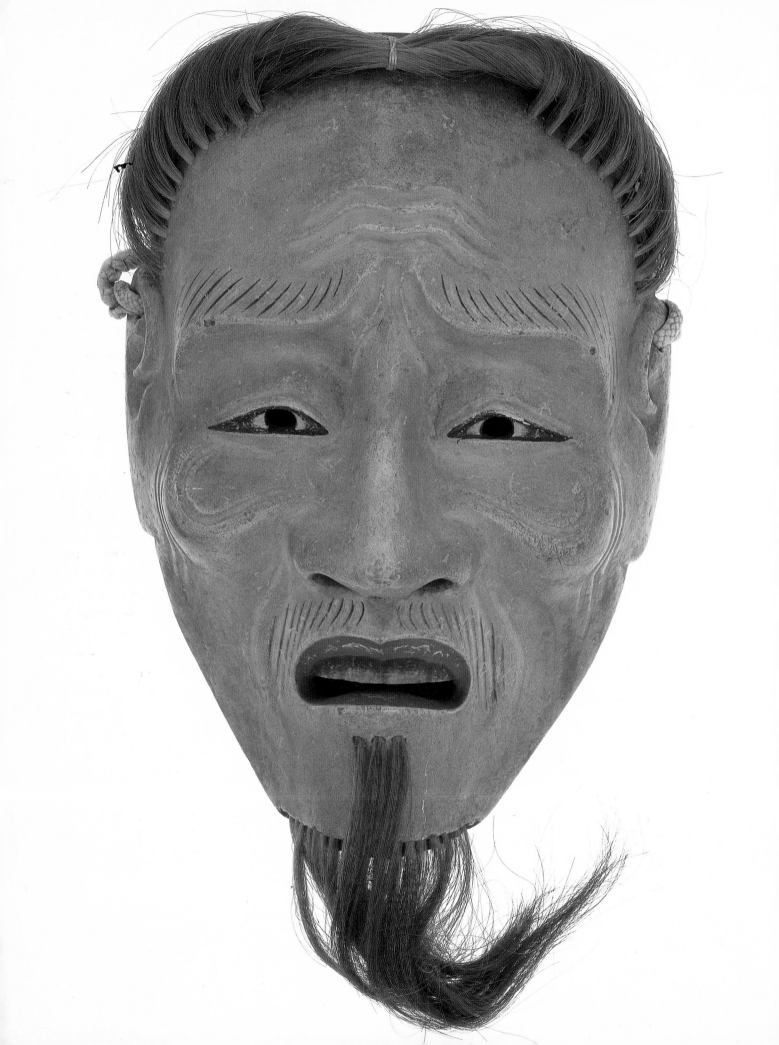

9. Japanese Nō mask of Kojō or Akobujō, an old man who features in several different roles. The mask of Kojō can be used for those plays in which a god manifests himself in earthly form, while that of Akobujō represents human beings in real-life tragedies. In the play *Tōsen*, a local Japanese ruler captures a Chinese ship and forces a crew member, Sokei Kanjin, to be his servant. Years later Sokei Kanjin's two children arrive bearing rich gifts for their father's freedom. By this time, however, he also has two Japanese children whom he cannot leave. He contemplates suicide, but his Japanese master shows mercy and allows him to leave with all four children. H. 21cm (without beard).

which can be the occasion for masking, as in many predominantly Catholic countries in Europe and Latin America. As Leach points out, the participation of masks may indeed survive as an aspect of such recurrent events even if their religious character alters or diminishes, when Holy Days become holidays.

In these cases then, some form of transformation, whether in status and personal circumstances or in calendrical events, is associated with masquerade, itself a transformational medium. Superficially, all seems tidy and explicable. Yet quite how the masker is involved in effecting these various transformations is by no means either straightforward or consistent. The temptation is to assume that it is the masker that somehow secures them. Some such direct relation may often and with justification be posited in those instances where masks are involved in healing rituals. This view is supported by the fact that in many cultures persons equipped with other capacities for transformation, such as an ability to switch in and out of a state of possession by spirits, are also credited with healing gifts. The transformation into an abnormal entity (the masked figure) or state (spirit possession) brings with it abnormal powers to transform the condition of others.

This is to make the mask crucial and central to the event. Often, however, it is not at all clear that this is so. On the African model, initiation is often a very lengthy and complex process which is not achieved in a single act. Initiates are usually removed from normal life for periods of months. The masker may only be involved at moments in the whole drawn-out procedure. Where, therefore, it is the ritual process that is the subject of interest, the participation of maskers can often virtually escape attention.

One of the most powerful interpretations of ritual is that developed by the anthropologist Victor Turner. Turner's discussion concentrated on the transitional or, in his vocabulary, the 'liminal' phase in ritual. This is an interim period in the whole process of ritual transformation characterised by ambiguous behaviour, a stage in the reclassifications taking place when former states are no longer operative and new ones are yet to be conferred. It is neither one thing nor another, a paradoxical period which is betwixt and between. Turner's discussion reflected his own experience among the Ndembu of Zambia. Here, masking is a part of male initiation. But Turner barely mentions this fact and offers no focused interpretation of the significance of masks; he describes them simply as monsters. The masks have been overlooked in the rush of pressing and complex rites which characterise the full range of procedures and need explanation. It is perhaps more accurate to say that the mask complements rather than necessarily brings about social transformation.

Even so, a number of commentators including Adams, Napier and Roberts, have at least sought to show how appropriate is this analysis of liminality to the interpretation of masking. Few would disagree. When maskers appear, their behaviour often does not immediately suggest that their purpose is either to lend tone and authority to the proceedings or to be explanatory and didactic. Groups of maskers appearing together can have quite different characteristics. Thus masks may run or dance about and their movements may be frenetic or graceful. Some are credited with remarkable agility. According to Bourgeois, the *kakungu* mask of the Yaka of Zaire is popularly supposed to be able to jump over houses and palm trees and to move around at great speed, feats which it shares with masks in many cultures. Some masks act aggressively, wielding sticks and lashing out alarmingly at onlookers, and some may be said to be imbued with such dangerous power that they cannot be touched by the uninitiated without contamination. Other masks, however, have a gentle disposition and mingle freely with spectators. Some are lewd, others restrained; some are deliberately and provocatively funny, others serious. Taken together any such group of masks make for an ambiguous and contradictory combination of behaviours.

Masks and theatrical performance

In these instances the masks perform to no set narrative. They move, gesture and dance; but they are not – certainly not in the Central African example quoted at more length – enacting a progressive and cumulative drama. They are not 'stage-managed'; indeed, although they may have attendants or helpers, in their unrestrained frenetic movement they often defy 'direction'. They have a dramatic impact but they are not, for all that, theatre.

However, despite the examples we have been looking at, general books on masks often see theatre as the proper context of masquerade, and the vocabulary of theatrical performance runs through the discussion of masking. Much of this, of course, derives from the association of masking with the development of Tragic and Comic theatre in the Ancient World, as discussed by Jenkins below. That dramatic tradition has now been reversed. In the Athenian tragic theatre masks were thought of as assisting portrayal by deploying well-established characteristics whose significance was readily interpreted by all as a particular generalised human condition. Alternatively, in the Comic theatre of the fifth century BC, individualising the mask allowed the actor more readily to satirise well-known Athenian personalities. Yet now the wearing of a mask is often seen more as a restriction to the talents of the actor than a help. A good performance communicates despite, rather than because of, the mask. But, as Jenkins points out, our emphasis on masks as disguise is at odds with the deployment of masks as an identification of character in Athenian theatre, what he calls 'face value' – the mask as revelation rather than concealment.

Thus critical discussion of several recent plays or films (such as, for example, John Hurt's performance in *The Elephant Man*) has often dwelled on the challenge of wearing a mask to the performance of leading actors used to communicating, in part at least, through facial expression. The contemporary actor, known for his or her performances in an unmasked state, succeeds by overcoming this limitation. The mask isolates, effaces; in the case of the Elephant Man, it imposes an identity that seems at times almost independent of the actor's efforts. Interestingly however, Greek and, most notably, traditional Japanese masked theatre both also had their renowned actors. The use of a mask was not an inevitable guarantee of the performer's anonymity, even though they did not also appear, as today's stage and screen actors, in unmasked performance.

Irvine gives (p. 145) a description of the preparations of the Japanese Nō performer before donning his mask. The performance itself is rendered more complex by the fact that the appearance of the mask, unlike those used in Greek theatre, is mostly expressionless or neutral. The stage is sparsely furnished; there are few props to assist in communicating or dramatising meaning. It is the actor's skill in gesture and suggestion which enlivens the performance. Before going on stage the performer studies his mask, thinking himself into his role by appropriating the personality he is to project.

In many African societies a somewhat comparable situation arises. Masquerades often involve the presentation of entities from the spirit world; yet in some the presence of the masker within the masquerade is common knowledge. There is an apparent paradox here, for it seems incompatible to accept the reality of the entity presented in masquerade and at the same time acknowledge the mechanics which bring it about. However, the possession of the masker by the spirit, which is part of African expectation of many masquerades, expels all implications of artificiality. Thus where Irvine is able to identify well-known historical Nō performers, as indeed Jenkins does for Ancient Greek masked theatre, Mack in discussing African masking ends by pointing out that there are few if any renowned African maskers. In the one case successful performance derives from the skill of the actor; in the other it is quite simply not a question of performance – the masquerade *is* spirit and becomes so in spite of, not because of, the performer.

Apart from directly theatrical masking, there are many other forms of masquerade whose didactic character gives them dramaturgical significance. In particular, masked parades in many parts of the world celebrate and interpret historical or mythical events. Those of Latin America discussed by Shelton are especially rich. We have mentioned above that the religious calendar provides a major occasion for masked pageant in many Catholic countries. The portrayals are frequently of Biblical characters. Yet

a specifically 'religious' character in this sense is also often hard to identify. Thus in Mexico, masquerades involving portrayals of the Conquistadors are numerous. Cortes and the Aztec ruler Montezuma often appear together with the Indian woman who was the Spaniards' interpreter (and reputedly Cortes' mistress) and a large cast of Indian and Spanish soldiery. Similarly the defeat of an invading French force by the Mexicans in 1862 is seen as a heroic moment in history appropriate to be celebrated each year on the day of the encounter, 5 May, in masked parades.

It is evident that in presenting the characters of the Conquest or nineteenth century battles a particular slant is given to history. The Conquest masquerades take place within the context of religious festivals. Although a link to specific Saints or Saints' Days is usually absent, the triumph of Christianity is none the less acknowledged. Thus pre-Conquest times are portrayed as a Golden Age, compromised by the catastrophe of the arrival of the Spanish, and only finally to an extent retrieved by the advent of the Christian faith. Re-enacting the events of the past converts historic remembrance into a vigorous tradition of the present. In the process different historical threads are frequently woven in together. This is not the history of the classroom and textbook but an inventive and eclectic theatrical gloss.

In Britain (and specifically in rural English counties) the performance of Mummers' Plays demonstrates the multilayered, indeed somewhat impenetrable, structure which a long tradition of practice can impart to pageant. This is a tradition which has now virtually disappeared though it remained a significant part of country festivals until after the Second World War. It was especially associated with the winter solstice and the vernal equinox, roughly Christmas and Easter. Discussion of Mummers' Plays is often atavistic; a link to a pre-Christian calendar and a source in more ancient peasant custom is frequently proposed, but ultimate origins remain uncertain. The Mummers passed down their traditions by word of mouth, recruiting new members to their company when one of their number retired. Until the structure of the plays began to be recorded, principally in the present century, it was only the lines and cues of the part an individual was specifically to perform that were taught. Inevitably different versions evolved among the various companies of players in different parts of the country.

The main characters as recorded by Whistler just after the Second World War provided an extraordinary pastiche of reference to historical and heroic figures. There were, for example, Father Christmas, King George, Bold Slasher or Turkey Snipe (or Knight), Quack Doctor, Twing-Twang or Little Johnny Jack, Rumour, Lawyer and Valiant Soldier. Some of these are straightforward to identify, though curiously juxtaposed. Thus King George is probably an eighteenth century transposition of a character who

10. Roman bronze mask, second century AD. Roman parade armour included a type of mask used in cavalry sports. These masks represent mythological characters and, although worn by men, could be male or female. This example, found in a tomb in Nola in Southern Italy, possibly portrays an Amazon. H. 25.2cm.

was originally Saint George, slayer of the dragon; Turkey Snipe is a reference to the 'Infidel' of the Crusades as in the lines 'In comes I the Turkey Snipe/ Come from my Turkish Land to fight'. Turkey Snipe challenges King George and is duly slain, though subsequently revived by the well-travelled Quack Doctor ('I've travelled India, South India and Bendigo . . . Itty-Titty where there's neither wall nor city').

Of the other characters, Father Christmas is a Victorian addition and appropriate to at least one of the seasons at which Mummers' Plays are traditionally performed. Twing-Twang is a reference to archers which the association with Little Johnny Jack suggests could be the Foresters of Sherwood, Little John or more probably Robin Hood himself. Certainly characters of heroic status have always been liable to verbal reference if not actual portrayal; for instance, the Mummers of Quidhampton in Wiltshire included the death of Nelson among their themes. Although many names and characters are thus explicable, the uncertain origins of some and the obscurity of many of the rhymes leads to the usage of the term mummery in English to mean 'buffoonery'.

Mummery, however, is also a synonym for 'masquerade'. The Mummers perform in costumes whose connection with the character of the portrayal is somewhat loose. The costume is composed of smocks or dresses with strips of cloth sewn all over and completed by a high, pointed headdress strung with streamers, like a maypole. Although no fixed mask with carved features is normally used, the result none the less is effectively to conceal the performer. As in many masking traditions elsewhere, identification with the character portrayed is not established by visual criteria alone – in the case of Turkey Snipe the verbal formula with which he introduces himself makes his identity as Turkey Snipe quite unequivocal, though an ultimate link to the Crusades would certainly escape most modern spectators.

Masks as emblems

Ceremonies rewarding excellence in acting on the stage or the screen often involve the presentation of a mask supported on a stand. Theatres often deploy images of masks on their programmes. Jenkins notes below that even in Ancient Greece coffins were sometimes adorned with mask-like images at their corners, though less perhaps as a tribute to the acting skill of the deceased than as an indulgence on the part of someone who regarded themselves as broadly cultured. Whatever the problems of presenting an artefact reserved essentially for use in performance through the static medium of a illustrated book, we get close to the idea of the mask as a separable icon in cases such as these where the mask becomes emblematic.

There are plenty of examples, apart from the manufacture of masks as tourist mementoes mentioned at the beginning, in which masks are made

11. Linen mummy mask of a woman, probably from Thebes, its date probably not earlier than the beginning of the second century AD. This is one of the most striking examples of the adoption of Hellenistic influences in southern Upper Egypt. H. 61cm.

other than for use in masquerade. The Lega of Zaire have taken the concept of the mask further than most. The anthropologist Daniel Biebuyck sums it up thus: 'Masks are used in an astonishing variety of ways. They are worn on the face, on the skull, on the back of the head, on the temples, near the shoulders, on the upper arms and on the knee; they are attached to a pole, fastened to a fence, or placed on the ground; they are swung around or dragged by their beards . . .'. Among the Lega, initiation into the various grades of a secret society involves the passing on of ever more esoteric knowledge, often about ways of behaving, in the form of verbal formulae which have to be learnt. Artefacts of many kinds, including masks, act as *aides-mémoire*, there being no necessary link between the form of the object and the moral lesson it sums up for those 'in the know'. Elsewhere in Central Africa, small ivory pendants in the form of masks are also made by the Pende and given to initiates who wear them strung round their necks. This is more than simply the employment of masks of suitable dimension as a kind of adornment, such as occurred with the famous Benin ivory and brass masks in Nigeria. The Pende ivories are both a badge of initiation and, it is said, a reminder of the teachings to which the initiate is now obliged to remain faithful. The Dan of the Ivory Coast produce miniature masks for comparable purposes.

These uses of course are individualised and related to the status or prestige of the initiate or the wearer. Yet masks may also be displayed in an emblematic way to indicate the character of an event. Among the Kuba of Zaire masking is an element in the initiation of boys into adulthood. Binkley makes the point that there are two separate traditions of initiation among the Kuba and that each has its own masking complex and associated songs and dances. Among the central Bushoong groups of the kingdom initiation takes place under royal patronage. Behind the Kuba king, however, lies the mythic figure of Woot, the first man of the Kuba, the first father and the first king. It was Woot who invented initiation. The basic myth in which this is established is given by the historian Jan Vansina: 'One day Woot, drunk with palm-wine . . . lay naked on the ground. His sons mocked him but his daughter found his loin-cloth and, walking backwards without looking at him, arranged it over his loins. When he awoke he rewarded his daughter by promising that her children would be heir (the origin of matrilineal succession) and punished his sons by sending them to initiation.' Initiation is a re-enactment of the punishment Woot inflicted on his sons to the point that initiates are told that they are Woot's sons, that they have offended their fathers and they are to be punished.

As Vansina and Binkley have noted, at the start of initiation the candidates pass through a large screen and leave the village for their seclusion in the forest; and at the conclusion of their passage into adulthood they ultimately emerge from behind it. The wall is also a kind of hoarding on

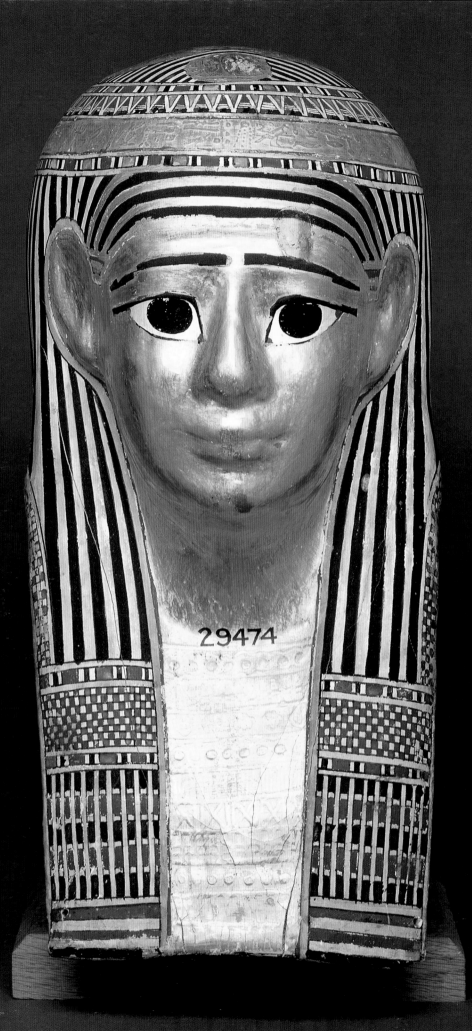

12. This cartonnage mummy mask exhibits features typical of the Ptolemaic period in Egypt, notably the gilded face with poorly defined anatomical features and the vivid colouring. Around the head is inscribed an abbreviated version of the 'spell for the mysterious head' (see p. 179). H. 48cm.

which are mounted a variety of emblems including natural objects, carved figures, animal traps and masks. Some of these document situations which occur in the course of initiation. Thus, a scene in which two francolins are displayed, a male caught in a snare and a female fluttering around him recalls the novices trapped in initiation and the girls excluded from their company. Others spell out the mythic context of the whole performance. On a central peak surmounting the wall is displayed the mask *yool* (the policeman) whose secret name is Woot. To either side are the mask *bwoom* and *mwash ambooy* which are identified with the two sons of Woot who were initially punished by being put through initiation. A fourth mask, *mboong a kwong*, is in the form of a seated man with an oversized penis, which is said to be a child of Woot, that is the novices themselves.

Although masks also perform in the course of initiation (as described by Mack in the first chapter), their display on the initiation wall provides a pastiche of reference to the complete mythic charter which underscores initiation. For those of the community not directly involved in the lengthy procedures of initiation, other perhaps than as anxious relatives of the initiates, they remain throughout the period as a token and marker of the events taking place in the forests beyond the fringes of the village. They are at once a division of space and a summation, through the display of appropriate emblems which include masks, of the authority under which Kuba boys are transformed into adults.

To say that masks can be emblematic is not therefore to say that they have become merely tokens, wrenched from an original context of meaning and significance and rendered impotent. Indeed all these cases document the reverse process. It is precisely because the masks have an authority and power in one context that they are meaningful in another, even if they are no longer worn in performance. The logical extension of these examples is a situation where masks have become too powerful in their own right for them to be safely worn at all even if their style of manufacture means that they could be. According to Brain, such a situation is found among the Bangwa of Cameroon. Here masks are carried on the shoulder by members of the Night Society. They have become too potent magically or mystically for them to be placed over the heads of humans.

None of the masks illustrated in this book, most drawn from the collections of the British Museum, are emblematic in any limited sense. Indeed each of the authors (also with two exceptions, drawn from the curatorial staff of the Museum, past and present) has sought to expand our insight into masking traditions generally rather than concentrating exclusively on the mask as such. Only Jenkins concentrates on a tradition where the mask is intended to be completely and unequivocally what it seems to be. Otherwise the world of masks is not a direct reflection of the real world but rather another form of reality. It is in two senses a world 'about face'.

13. Wood mask, Punu, Gabon. This mask is one of the earliest collected in a style associated with the performance of funerary rites in southern Gabon. The polychrome nature of the mask contrasts with others known from the area (and probably of later creation) which are characteristically white-faced. They are said to be in some sense portraits of the deceased.
H. 29cm.

AFRICAN MASKING

Africa is often supposed to be a – perhaps even *the* – major centre of the world's masking traditions. In reality this assumption has little to do with any detailed popular knowledge of the extent of masking practice on the continent; arguably it is, rather, a vague lingering impression traceable to the 'discovery' of African masks and sculpture by Picasso and others at the beginning of this century. What could be seen in the studios of Paris at the time was principally from areas of French colonial interest. Even so, masks have come to be regarded as emblematic of African culture in general.

Such external views of African indigenous life are potent sources of misunderstanding. In this case, however, the most basic assumption is to an extent correct – some form of masking is indeed very widespread in Africa, at least in areas to the south of the Sahara. Masks seen out of context give an unbalanced impression. Most are carved of wood and are

14. Fibre mask, Tiriki, Kenya. After circumcision, male initiates among the Tiriki don masks which are used both in ceremonies and to hide the initiate when obliged to appear in public during the period of the rite of passage. It is said that should other people see his face in this period of transition the initiate would become diseased. L. 140cm.

from West Africa or the Equatorial Forests. Yet in these areas and elsewhere there are many masks which are constructed of less durable materials (see fig. 14) – grasses, leaves, bark, feathers, cloth – and many which are not subject to any special procedures to preserve them but are simply destroyed when they are no longer required. Their ephemeral nature makes them that much more difficult to document. But such masks are used in comparable circumstances to those that are carved and sculpted and, from an anthropological perspective, are the same thing. When these masks are included a significant range of cultures from Eastern and Southern Africa, where masking is not otherwise thought to be extensive, come into consideration.

Masks of leaves and feathers are, of course, somewhat shapeless constructions. The question of the extent to which masks are deliberate artistic creations portraying specific identifiable subjects is another complicated issue. Where a carved mask is used, it may seem that the purpose of the masquerade is to represent an entity of one particular kind and none other. In fact, as we shall see, the question of the identity of any masked performance is in itself a vexed one. Yet, an all-embracing costume appears to raise no such questions of aesthetics and identity as a sculpted mask. Ephemeral masks may, it seems, simply conceal the masker without seeking to represent any other entity, human or otherwise. To that extent they are like the veils of Islamic cultures in North Africa. Again the impression is often misleading.

Most masks are assumed to have ritual significance, however defined. The use of masks for amusement or fun seems most clearly to be associated with the western world where the continuing employment of masks in overtly religious or ritual circumstances is limited. There are, however, equivalent situations in Africa. In Somalia, Clarke has reported masks in use by some Muslim populations, among whom masking is not a frequent phenomenon (though found extensively among West African converts to Islam as reported in detail by Bravmann). A more distant hint that masks were once used by Somali in rain-making ceremonies, in healing and as a cure for sterility in women is suggested, but these purposes had been completely forgotten by the dancers of such masks interviewed in the 1950s. Similarly in Madagascar, where masking is not otherwise known, the author has occasionally seen Mahafaly use wood masks 'to amuse/ frighten the children of the village'.

In reality any masked performance has a complex of purposes, and even the most 'serious' are not without their humorous, entertaining aspects. Many masks appear together or successively, each having a distinctive and different character, from the awesome to those which mimic, poke fun, and satirise (see fig. 16). Masking performances can without discrepancy be both serious ritual and captivating entertainment. Even masks that act aggressively towards spectators do not want for an audience. And all,

15. Wood mask with large metal ring, Makonde, Mozambique. Most of the masks used by the Makonde are quite precise in subject – facial scarification applied using wax permits association of the mask with particular groups of individuals. Exotic subjects are rare. Here, however, the headdress, ring and tufts of hair on the chin and the head suggest a Muslim trader originating from one of the many Arab-Swahili communities on the East African Coast. The mask is worn high on the head with the eyes focusing down on the spectators. H. 35cm.

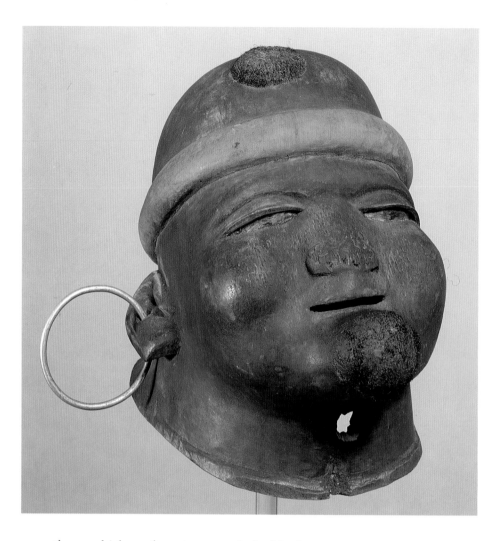

16. Wood mask with string attachments and a printed cloth shawl, Chewa, Malawi. The Chewa use masks in the ceremonies conducted by the *nyau* society, a male organisation which, among other activities, oversees funerary rites. Nyau masks are of two basic types, one which represents the dead and a second which portrays wild animals. Within these categories, however, a certain amount of eclecticism is apparent. Masks representing Europeans are common. The mask may verge on caricature, seeking to recall particular individuals by emphasising well-known physical features (here those of a local missionary). H. 25cm.

even those which perform in an entirely frivolous manner, may be equally regarded as emanations from the spirit world rather than actors in extravagant disguise.

Clearly, when the masking traditions of Africa as a whole are considered there are so many variations of style, materials, use, behaviour and occasions for masking, that in a short chapter definitive discussion will be impossible. It has seemed better, therefore, to select a number of themes and attempt to describe them with reference to well-discussed examples rather than to try and mention all (even all the most vigorous and better discussed) masking traditions of the continent.

Myth and history

The suggestion that masking is deeply embedded in African culture also, of course, raises questions as to its origins. A common assumption is that the tradition of African masking may be of considerable antiquity. Even excluding the evidence from Ancient Egypt, which is the subject of a separate chapter, there are other pointers to the past usage of masks. In the

17. Wood mask in the form of a bush cow with stuffed raffia horns and raffia fibre fringe, Zombo, Zaire/Angola borders. Masks in this general style are found among a number of Eastern Kongo peoples, on the Zombo plateau and into the Kwango-Kwilu river area where they are most notably associated with the Yaka. Masks are used in male initiation ceremonies, the secrets of masquerade being a primary subject of the initiation process. H. 26cm.

18. Wood mask, Guro, Ivory Coast. This mask appears to be in a form which mixes animal and human attributes and is associated with spirits of the bush. H. 27cm.

Sahara, an area not nowadays associated with masking of any kind, there is some evidence that masks were once in use. The famous Tassili rock paintings include an apparent representation of a mask style, dating admittedly from a period when the Sahara was much less arid than is the case today. The style in fact is intriguingly similar to that found today in some masks to the south of the Equatorial Forest in Zaire and Angola. A direct link of any kind however, is very unlikely as, apart from the geographical disparities involved, the paintings seem to have been executed upwards of 4,000 years ago.

Similarly, the rock paintings of the San (otherwise known as the Bushmen) in the Drakensburg mountains of South Africa include masked figures. The masks in these cases are animal skins and heads which conceal hunters and thereby enable them to approach their prey. This more pragmatic use extends the roster of occasions to which masking is appropriate. As most masks in Africa are made of perishable organic materials, such evidence from both northern and southern Africa, though it tells us nothing about ultimate origins (nor could be expected to), at least supports the view that masking is not a recent phenomenon.

Many African masking traditions, of course, also have their own mythical foundations known to many members of the communities involved. In some societies myth provides a kind of template for masked events. Reference has been made in the Introduction to the initiation wall of the Kuba in Zaire with its emblematic masks. Initiation is associated with the origin myth of the Kuba which relates, as we saw, the conception of the Kuba from the incestuous relationship of the original ancestor, Woot, and his sister. The Bushoong, the ruling group of the Kuba kingdom, also retain histories of the migration which brought them to their present location to the south of the Kasai River.

Vansina and Binkley have both described how, at the start of initiation, the candidates first pass through the initiation wall erected at the end of the village. Behind this an underground passage has been dug. The tunnel has several niches set into its sides and through it the novices (babyeen, people of the tunnel) must crawl one by one as they depart for their seclusion in the forest. They are stripped of their clothes and, having passed through the wall, are confronted by Nnup, a masker carrying a ritual knife and other royal insignia and wearing leopard skin, the prerogative of the king under whose auspices initiation takes place. Nnup stands with legs astride so that his leopard-skin skirt covers the entrance to the tunnel. As the initiates pass between his legs they disappear from view into the passage on a journey which, like a trip on a ghost train, carries them through a series of fearful experiences. In advance they have been told how they will be confronted by a leopard whose growls they hear from its underground lair, and they will pass over a river in which many will drown.

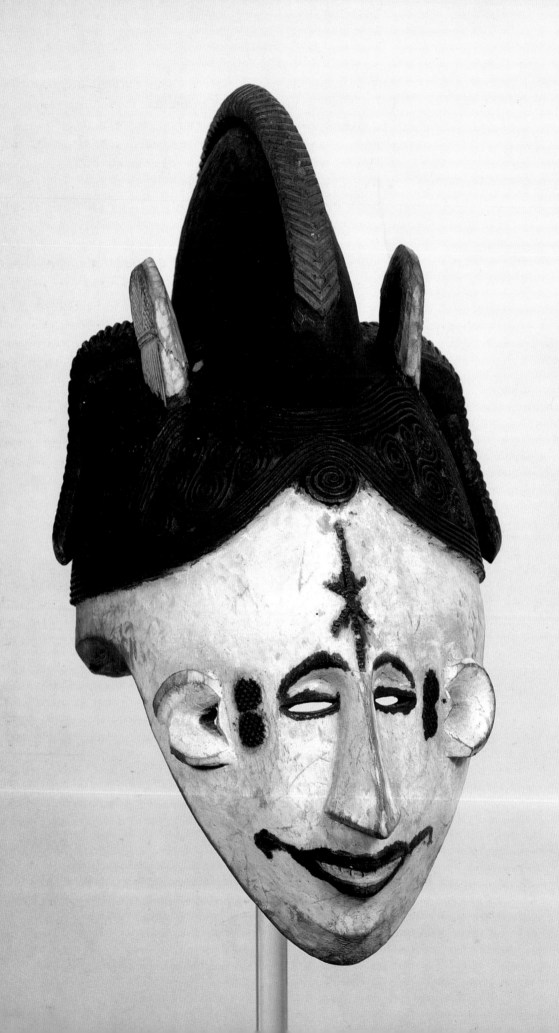

19. Wood mask, Ibo, Nigeria. Ibo masking traditions are complex. A basic division, however, exists between white-faced masks, as here, and black or red masks. The former are regarded as beautiful, serene, usually feminine, by contrast with the fierce, sometimes horned, darkened masks which act aggressively. H. 37cm.

Their chances of escaping unscathed are slim. At the first of the recesses within the passage they are pounced on by two men; next they approach the leopard itself where they discover that it is only a man producing a low droning sound on a friction drum. As each in turn passes along the route they come next upon a blacksmith hammering in another recess. Then they fall into a ditch of water before emerging at the other end between the legs of the mask Kalengl. Kalengl is a female mask, the mother of initiation.

The sense in which this sequence of events enacts a mythic charter is evident. The two masks are associated with Woot and his sister/wife, and the novices are the Kuba themselves, the product of their incestuous union. They enter the tunnel naked as children and are symbolically reborn at the other end crawling from between the legs of the female mask. The leopard is Woot, whose roar (the friction drum) has been heard in the village in the nights preceding the disappearance of the novices from public view. The blacksmith is also Woot, as in the Kuba aphorism 'the hoes Woot first forged were the feet of men'. The water is the source of life and in myth the starting point of the migrations of the Bushoong (the central ethnic group of the Kuba kingdom) which led them to their present home. Indeed the tunnel in a sense is itself a kind of mask for the process of ingestion and transformation of initiates.

Masks and gender

In such cases myth provides a kind of script which directs the course of ritual. Elsewhere, however, myth reflects on the origin of masking itself, often relating it in the form of historical narrative. There may also be separate 'histories' of many individual masks. Like all such narrative, the content can be interpreted in a number of different ways beyond simple story-telling. The associated mythology, like the masking itself, may amplify, refer to, provoke, dramatise a variety of issues. Given the local sources of such themes, it is interesting that many share a somewhat similar structure.

For instance, Picton informs us that among the Ebira in Nigeria contemporary opinion has it that 'God made things double; masquerading for men and witchcraft for women'. The provinces of men and of women are clearly distinguished and indeed ranged against each other: *eku*, the term for masquerading, also refers to powers inherited from the world of the ancestors among which is the ability to counteract premature death by witchcraft. This situation is in line with much other evidence from Africa. Writing of masking along the Gambia River in 1730, Francis Moore described a masquerader (a 'Mumbo Jumbo, an Idol') thus: 'This is a Thing invented by the Men to keep their Wives in awe, who are so ignorant (or at least pretend to be so) as to take it for a Wild Man'. The Gelede masquerades

of the Yoruba of Nigeria embody outrageous portrayals of women and reversals of the normal relationships of men and women which obtain in human society. This is not, however, to imply that women are a suitably passive subject of satire, weak and defenceless inhabitants of the undemanding margins of society who can be ridiculed without fear of reprisal. The whole structure of Gelede is animated and intensified by the paradox that, although men manipulate many of the structures of action, they fear the hidden powers of women.

Generally men control, own and dance masks, even if the masks sometimes represent women; they alone know its secrets and articulate its powers. Given this, it is remarkable how many masking societies identify

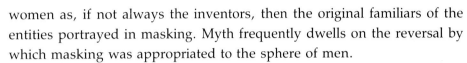

20. Wood helmet mask, Mambila, Nigeria/Cameroon borders. A common feature of many societies in the grassfields of Cameroon and along the country's western borders is the presence of an elephant society which conducts masquerades. In some cases, as among the Bamileke, the mask is a beaded construction. Here, a wood mask liberally interprets the elephant form. L. 90cm.

women as, if not always the inventors, then the original familiars of the entities portrayed in masking. Myth frequently dwells on the reversal by which masking was appropriated to the sphere of men.

The Kalabari Ijo live in the creeks and rivers of the Niger Delta. Their masquerades are associated with water spirits and exclusive to men. Yet the Ekine Society, which controls masking, is named after a woman. The basic myth concerns Ekinabe, a beautiful young woman from one of the delta towns who was abducted by the dancing water spirits and taken in captivity to their home beneath the waters. Horton continues:

> The mother of the water spirits was angry at what they had done, and commanded her children to take Ekinabe back to the land of men. Before returning her, however, each water spirit showed her its special play; and when she returned to her home, she taught the people all the plays she had seen. The plays became very popular and were constantly performed. But the young men found it difficult to obey a certain rule which the water spirits had imposed on her . . . After they had disobeyed this rule three times, the water spirits lost patience and took Ekinabe away for good. Since then, men have taken her as the patron goddess of the masquerade.

Further to the west, across a wide area from Sierra Leone to the Ivory Coast, the leading institution associated with masking is the secret society known as Poro. Poro members assume responsibility for a range of important matters including education and conduct, political and economic affairs and the administration of magical medicine. Their authority in part comes from the control they exercise over spirits, as witnessed by their ability to orchestrate spirits in masquerade. Poro is the quintessential male society, contrasted in a number of areas with the female association known as Sande (or Sandogo). Yet it is striking that, among the Senufo of the Ivory Coast, it is women who underscore and endorse the authority of Poro. Thus, discussing the part of Poro masks in funerals, Glaze perceptively notes that 'a telescopic vision that understandably focuses on the visual excitement of masquerades in a Senufo funeral ritual is apt to miss the

21. Wood helmet mask, Mende, Sierra Leone. Of the masks illustrated in this chapter this is the only one to be owned and used exclusively by women, those of the female Sande society. In local iconographic understanding its features are associated with aspects of feminine ideals of beauty. H. 44cm.

older women standing unobtrusively at the periphery of the ritual arena, yet it is the very presence of the Sandogo leaders that both validates and adds power to the ritual itself'. Women, female ancestors, have a greater ideological weight than men (as is reflected also in the fact that in set piece sculptures which show the primordial couple the female is always portrayed as larger). In the secret language of Poro initiates there is a common phrase used as a password and formal greeting which translates as 'at our mother's work'. The true head of Poro turns out to be a woman.

Masks and identity

It is important to emphasise these mythic foundations, for in practice one of the few masking institutions where masks are actually owned and danced exclusively by women is in the Sande Society, which is especially strong among the Mende of Sierra Leone. Sande is concerned with the initiation of women into adulthood and is thus widespread in those communities which have it (though the related Sandogo Society in the Ivory Coast serves other purposes and is not so all-embracing in its membership).

The question of what the mask portrays or represents was raised at the start of this chapter. Sande masks provide a good point at which to return to this issue. Expressing the Mende perspective, the anthropologist Jedrej says, 'in this instance it is the concealing mask that is quite unambiguously identified as the spirit . . . the appearance of the Sande spirit is wholly representational; it is spirit'. What is suggested is that masking is not so much a portrayal as an actual embodiment. The emphasis is not so much on the act of concealment (the masker) as on the act of revelation (the presentation of spirit). All Sande masks are very much the same, share iconographical features and are regarded as of equal status, such differences as there are being the result of local variations in carving style rather than the place of masks in any hierarchy of forms and styles (see fig. 21).

The Mende concept of spirits (*ngafanga*) ranges over a variety of different entities from conceptions of the human soul to dangerous spirits of the forest. One such is the dancing spirits which by contrast with others are visible and appear in villages as dancers, acrobats and jesters. Like masked figures these are also distinctive in another way. Any accidental encounter with spirits in their natural habitat – the forest – transforms the individual who as a result becomes insane, or very rich, or a healer. It is appropriate that initiation also takes place in the seclusion of the forest, the place of mysterious transformations. When they appear in the village, however, spirits are rendered harmless. If it were otherwise, and a confrontation with a mask in the village were of the same order as that with a spirit in the bush, then, to follow Mende logic, villages would be variously populated by mystics, millionaires, and medical practitioners. In masquerade

the spirit itself is transformed and in that act is robbed of its power to transform the onlooker.

A contrast to this is provided by the Central African example of *makishi* discussed in the Introduction. There masks were concerned with male initiation and were identified as the dead resurrected to participate in a particular set of events (see fig. 22). At the same time, however, individual masks carry names which also identify them with stock figures of various kinds: with wealthy aristocrats, stern or impotent figures, attractive young women and so forth. Although these identifications are quite precise, exactly how they relate to the equally firm association of masquerade with the dead is less clear.

To complicate matters further, the expectations of the audience of this cast of masks is far from uniform. Some are greeted with fearful anxiety, others anticipated with eager excitement. Similarly, while Sande masks show minimal iconographic variation, the external features of each makishi are often distinctive of each particular portrayal. Some masks are of wood, others of barkcloth. Some display considerable naturalism, others are relatively abstract; and many, though associated with the world of the dead, are not even limited to human subjects. Thus, for instance, the anthropologist Victor Turner reports an Ndembu mask which is part human and is partly intended as a depiction of a grassy plain, while Gluckmann witnessed a Wiko masquerade, also in Zambia, which portrayed mats of grass floating on a river, this part of a collection of masks otherwise identified with 'cannibals of the forest, animals, sorcerers' familiars, dead men turned into animals, foreigners . . .'. Among the Zambian Chewa, Yoshida even found his fieldwork vehicle rendered as a kind of architectural mask in reeds but with the correct number plate. Such representations seem in the end to be more directed towards distinguishing between characters in a specific repertoire of masks than adhering closely to any circumscribed idea of what masks might be about.

Perhaps the clearest statement of the ethnography of makishi is White's description of Lovale masking in Zambia. The crucial Lovale statement about the identity of masks is the phrase *natuya nakusangula likishi*, literally 'we are going to bring to life a *likishi*'. The verb refers specifically to resurrection from the grave; but it does not refer to the bringing to life of ancestral spirits. Masks do not represent ancestors – not only are these invisible, but in any case they do not reside in graves. The verb is used rather of were-creatures, monsters ill-disposed to the human world, such as a man who returns from the dead as a beast of prey. A similar implication seems to be present in the vocabulary used by Chokwe and Lunda in Angola and Zaire, for whom an act of 'resurrection' is likewise the prelude to masquerade (and incidentally this also applies to the Chewa on the Zambia/Malawi borders, as Yoshida has pointed out). White notes that the Lovale masks

23. Wood mask, Kwele, Gabon. In northern Gabon, the home of the Kwele, masks are associated with cults dedicated to counteracting the destructive aspect of witchcraft. H. 26.5cm.

22. Mask of painted bark and resin and with fibre netting, Chokwe, Angola. Chokwe masks show a variety of named and distinct types each with its characteristic behaviour. This is the mask Kalelwa, one deeply associated with the world of the spirits, which appears in the context of male circumcision. Representations of Kalelwa also appear in other contexts, for example on chiefly chairs. H. 76cm.

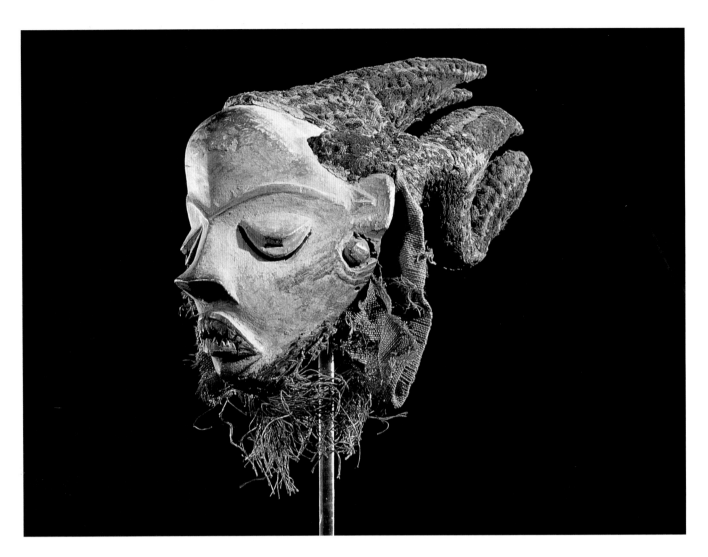

24. Wood mask with fibre attachment, Pende, Zaire. This mask appears to be an example of the type known as *phumbu*, the murderer, one of the large cast of masks appropriate to different phases of Pende initiation. H. 21cm.

katotoji, *chikaza*, and *ngondo* all have names that are otherwise applied to the familiars of sorcerers. These details help explain other aspects of the use of masks in circumcision rites in Central Africa. Thus non-initiates touching makishi are said to contract serious illness; in some places it is considered dangerous even to walk on ground on which masks have recently danced; and when initiation is at an end, the masks are burned. The occurrence of the same root *kisi* for both masquerade and, especially in the Lower Congo area, to denote objects and substances imbued with magical power adds further support to this interpretation of makishi.

Of course not all masks are regarded as equally 'dangerous'. Often masks form a community which taken together present a range of differing characteristics. Kubik has noted that among the Mbwela in Angola they are thought of as comprising a kind of court hierarchy with king, courtiers and retinue, depending on the powers which they are perceived to possess. Among the Pende in Zaire de Sousberghe has described two types of mask which appear during the course of circumcision rites. *Minganji* are worn

25. Wood mask with fibre attachment, Pende, Zaire. This mask was one of several collected by the ethnographer Emil Torday in 1909. It seems to be an example of the mask known as *tundu*, one of the more playful masks which mingles readily with women and children and comes back repeatedly to mimic other masks that perform. H. 21.5cm.

by the overseers of the circumcision camp where initiation is effected. By contrast *mbuya* are danced in the course of the festivities which accompany the return of the candidates to their villages. Both categories, like the makishi to which they are related, are associated with the dead (*mvumbi*) though the connection is weaker in the case of mbuya. Thus, whereas minganji are regarded as sinister, as affairs of magic, mbuya are more playful and theatrical, interacting more directly with the onlookers.

Mbuya masks are also more numerous than minganji. Gangambi's discussion of the types known from just one district of Pendeland lists as many as thirty-one distinct characters as the subjects of separate representations ranging from persons with physical disabilities, such as hunchbacks, to coquettes, stilt walkers and missionaries. No individual masked event perhaps ever includes the complete cast of mbuya characters. Nevertheless with so many potential subjects it is no wonder that the mask and costume itself is frequently insufficient clue to the identity of a particular performer. If we are seeking visual criteria to such identification it is sometimes to the

26. Wood mask with a central crest, astride which stands a female figure, Bobo Fing, Burkina Faso. A mask made and worn by smiths at funerals and at initiations. H. 69.5cm.

various props the masker may employ and to his characteristic gesture, style of movement, song or voice that we must look. Giketshiketshi, the missionary, is known less by his mask as such than by his straw hat with a wide brim; Pikasa, the buffalo, typically runs four paces before lashing out in the direction of the spectators, and from time to time pours out a stream of mud from a concealed sack in imitation of excrement.

Ultimately, however, the spectators know which character is performing because they are told. The first mask to appear is always *tundu*, an obscene comedian who introduces the spectacle to follow. Once he has performed he remains on the scene acting as a kind of master of ceremonies, imitating or parodying the masks which are to come or accompanying their performance. Each successive mask is supported by its own attendants who appear on the dance ground in advance of the mask itself. Its distinctive 'signature tune' is beaten on the drums while the group of accompanists announce its arrival with songs explaining what it represents, how it is to move, and extolling the forthcoming artistry.

The situation among the Kalabari Ijo is still more extreme. There are

28. Wood helmet mask, Senufo, Ivory Coast. Wood masks are used by the Senufo in the ceremonial of the Poro society, a widespread initiation society in West Africa. This type of mask is often referred to as a 'firespitter', a reference to the much-quoted but perhaps uncommon practice of Poro maskers blowing sparks from the mouth of the mask in performance. L. 45cm.

27. (*opposite*) Wood mask with fibre attachment, Dogon, Mali. Masks of this type (*walu*) are used both at funerary and at agricultural rites. They are said to represent a large antelope, though their form is also reflected in the architectural style of sanctuaries. H. 60cm.

between thirty and fifty water spirits that appear in the cycle of masked dancers. Members of the Ekine go to distant creeks in canoes to summon water spirits to attend the performances with which they are associated, retracing, as it were, the captive journey and return to the world of spirits of the patroness of their society, Ekinabe. Water spirits are not held to have a fixed form. They are generally said (by Horton, for example) to possess affinity both with animals and with human beings. When they materialise, however, it is most often by taking the form of a water-creature, usually a python or crocodile, though sharks, sawfish, skate or jellyfish are also appropriate vessels of water spirits. These associations can be the basis of sculptural forms with references to the scales or patterning on the skin of such creatures being applied to the surface of objects, or the creature itself carved in relief. Many of the representations used in masquerade incorporate such features in combination with the human head. Thus a schematised carving of human eyes and nose may be completed, in the most familiar examples, by projections recalling the jaws of a crocodile. Whether or not these external features are sufficient to bear the burden of identification with water spirits, the fact that the mask is in fact worn on the top of the head with its features facing upwards suggests that visual criteria are not the sole and most compelling reference. Travelling to distant creeks and dedicating these headpieces to particular water spirits is at least as important in securing their identity.

In this context the vocabulary Kalabari use of the association between

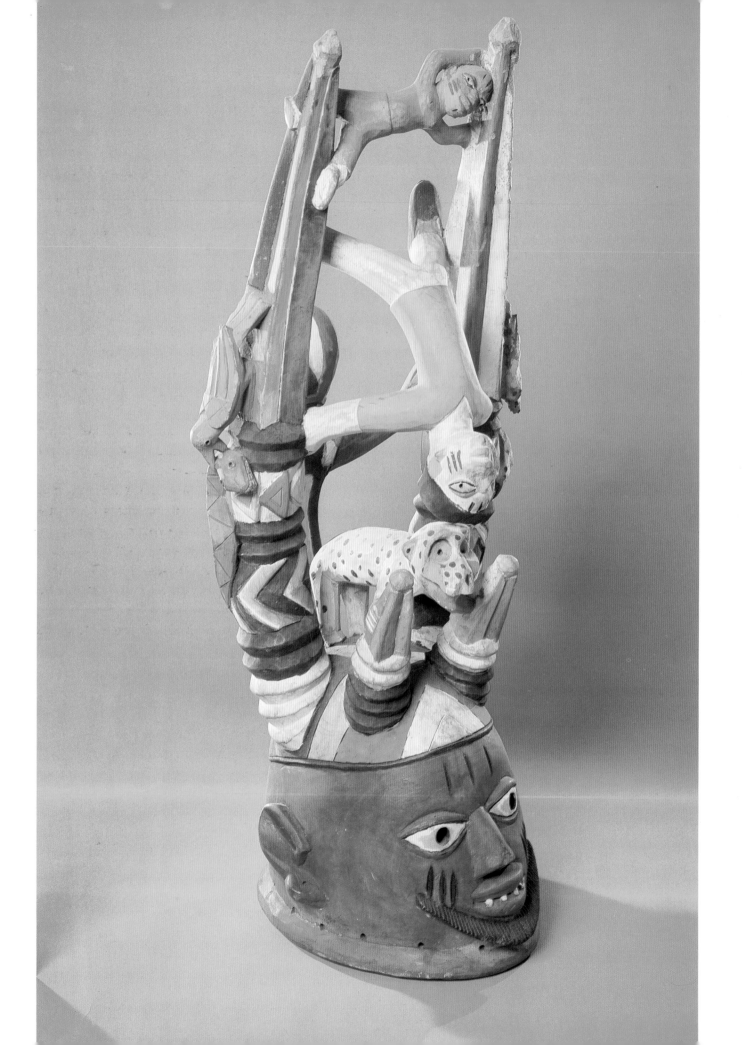

water spirit and masquerade is revealing. Where a mask or headpiece is used – and they are not invariably a part of the masquerade costume – it is referred to as the 'name' of the masquerade while the rest of the costume is just decoration. This certainly gives the mask a separable significance; it is through its agency that the relationship between performance and particular spirits is secured. Yet, in practice, this identity is brought out by the characteristic drum rhythms and dance movements distinctive of each play, and it is to this, not to the form of the mask, that an Ekine member refers when asked how he recognises the subject of a particular performance. Bearing the same name is not necessarily the same thing as bearing concrete physical likeness. Further, the mask is talked of as being 'owned' by the water spirit to which it is dedicated, and 'ownership' stresses the authority by which the performance takes place rather than specific details of the portrayal. Finally, during the performance itself the water spirit is said to 'walk with' the Ekine dancer, a turn of phrase which once more serves to distance the portrayal achieved in masquerade from the entity portrayed.

We end, therefore, where we started; there is no single model which encapsulates the variety of African masking practice. The issue is not whether spectators know the identity of the masker, or even acknowledge that there is a masker articulating the performance from within the concealing artifice of the mask. It is the mask and not the masker which is the point, the performance and not the performer. Where the carver of the mask might in some societies be an artist reputed for his skills, the masker is perhaps never renowned separately from the masquerade. Certainly it is unlikely to be his (or her) identity that establishes the identity of the masquerade. How that is achieved may often require reference to detailed and variable aspects of the masquerade as a whole, of which the visible appearance of the mask is one.

29. Wood mask, Yoruba, Nigeria. *Egungun* masks, of which this is an example, are found throughout Yorubaland where they appear at annual festivals. They are associated with lineage ancestors and as such may also be brought out at times of crisis when sustaining ancestral vitality is asserted. This example, from Abeokuta, echoes another Yoruba mask form, that of *Gelede*. H. 72.5cm.

MASKS IN OCEANIA

Melanesia

Masks in Oceania are characteristic of, and virtually limited to, Melanesia, which is an area of masks par excellence. In almost every major island group masks were made and used in various elaborate religious ceremonial cycles or events performed in connection with rites of initiation (into adulthood, cults, secret societies or combinations of these), mortuary rites and celebrations of the agricultural cycle.

Melanesian masks are associated with the world of men, the institutionalised expressions of which are men's associations involving men's houses, spirit cults and secret and/or graded societies, from which women are excluded. Men are the mask-makers and performers. Even though some masks represent female supernatural beings, it is always men who are the actors, never women. The contribution of women, who proclaim themselves (and are believed by men) to be ignorant of the true nature of the masquerade, is indirect. They may provide some materials for the manufac-

30. *Malanggan* mask from New Ireland, Papua New Guinea. These characteristic helmet masks invariably have a high dome with a crest of yellow vegetable fibre; each half of the dome is decorated in different fashion, as in this example. The painted ornamentation of the face is also asymmetrical. H. 41cm.

31. Mask from Ambrym, Vanuatu. Made from palm spathe, painted and decorated with 'blond tresses' of vegetable fibre. According to the accompanying information, it was 'worn during dances . . . which take place during the pig feasts'. H. 62cm (excluding fringe).

ture of masks and costumes; they are involved in the production of food and rearing of pigs which, together with valuables, are necessary for feasts and exchanges which play a crucial role in the ceremonies; and they constitute an audience. They are also seen by men as a potential threat to their hold on the spiritual world through their reproductive power. The need for secrecy from, and the exclusion of, women is justified in some societies by myths which tell of women as the original owners of the masks from whom the objects themselves, and their secrets and powers, have been appropriated by men.

Melanesian masks vary greatly in their forms and complexity. The human face is the predominant form but animal masks also occur, and nearly all masks have additional decoration of feathers, shells and other materials, and mantles, capes or skirts of leaves. In some cases it is difficult to make a distinction between an elaborate headdress and a mask proper which hides the face, and not all masks are intended to conceal the identity of the wearer. Some of them can be made by any qualified adult male, others demand the skills of specialists whose individual talents are recognised and valued, and whose services are sought after.

Many Melanesian masks were meant to be ephemeral, made for one particular occasion and then discarded, either because having fulfilled their purpose they were of no further use, or because they were ritually dangerous and had to be destroyed. Those which have been preserved in museum collections, very often without their full costume and ornaments, and seen out of context, are poor shadows of their former selves, bereft of vitality and, to some extent, of meaning.

In some instances the precise significance and function of masks is now impossible to establish. The societies which produced them have been so efficiently 'missionised' that the old knowledge has to be painstakingly reconstructed from old sources, often scanty, fragmentary and contradictory, and from surviving traditions and beliefs, often already altered and diluted.

Some types of masks are no longer made, especially those which, like the huge masks of the Elema (see below), required remarkable skills and enormous resources for their manufacture. Others are still produced. Some are continuations of old traditions, others are expressions of a revival of traditions. They are used either in a traditional context or integrated into a new one, often that of church-associated activities, or they may simply be part of a performance lending a festive air to local events of importance.

ISLAND MELANESIA

New Caledonian masks, which existed only in the north and the centre of the main island, are made of wood, boldly carved and stained black (see fig. 32). Those from the north are carved emphatically in the round, elon-

32. Mask from New Caledonia. Face carved from wood, human hair and beard; at the back of the head is a vegetable-fibre plaited band from which a feather mantle would have been suspended, and of which only some feathers remain. H. 66cm.

gated, with a huge beak-like nose overhanging the mouth, whereas those from the central area are round and flattish, with a short nose. It is not entirely clear what precise function the masks had in the traditional New Caledonian culture. It seems that the northern area masks symbolised the power of the chiefs and appeared in mourning ceremonies following the death of a man of rank; those from the central area simply provided entertainment. In addition, a number of masks in museum collections are known to have specific names which probably represent various incarnations of the deity associated with water and the underworld.

In Vanuatu masks are numerous and varied (see fig. 31). Some are associated with ceremonies connected with graded societies, prevalent in the area, in which a man obtains promotion to a higher social and religious rank through increasingly larger payments of pigs. Others are used in dances in which mythological or everyday events are re-enacted. The distinction between masks and headdresses is here particularly difficult to make. Such masks/headdresses are often conical but diamond-shaped and oval masks also occur. They may be modelled in composite vegetable-fibre paste or made of palm spathe, bark, or spider's web. On Pentecost, Ambrym and Malekula wood masks are found, and those made of hard wood are sculpturally the most interesting, with strongly modelled features and hooked noses somewhat reminiscent of New Caledonian masks.

Masks are still made in Vanuatu: for traditional ceremonies, for dances accompanying special occasions such as the opening of a new church or a local art festival, and for sale to visitors.

A special type of mask, no longer made, was found in the Banks and Torres Islands of Vanuatu. It is interesting not so much for its aesthetic appeal – it is a simple painted head-and-face covering – as for its association with mens' secret societies, each with its own symbols and costumes, which were widespread and numerous in these islands. Not a great deal of precise information about these societies, called *Tamate*, has been recorded but we know that initiation was through payments and involved a period of seclusion. Membership conferred the privilege of wearing a mask and, in this guise, the right to execute fines for transgressions of rules imposed by the society. As an instrument of social control they have much in common with the *Dukduk* societies of Eastern New Britain (see below).

In the Solomon Islands masks are rare. They are found in Vanikoro of the Santa Cruz group – where, as Rose suggests, they are probably related to the Tamate cults of the Banks and the Torres Islands – and in the northwest (Nissan, Buka and Bougainville). But even though masks are not characteristic of most of the traditional societies of the Solomons, one of the most typical souvenirs a visitor may acquire in the Islands today is a wood mask, carved from dense light-coloured wood and decorated with pearl-shell inlay. A story, perhaps apocryphal, has it that some years ago,

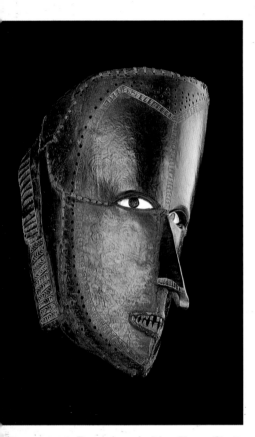

33. Funeral mask, Mer, Torres Strait Islands. Made of turtle shell, with white shell eyes and incised decoration filled with lime. Similar anthropomorphic masks from Erub are usually embellished with hair, moustache and beard of string or human hair. H. 41cm.

34. Mask from Saibai, Torres Strait Islands. Made of wood, with low-relief painted decoration, shell eyes, and eyebrows and hair of vegetable fibre (note the little turtle figure at the chin). Used in ceremonies associated with the ripening of the *ubar* fruit (a variety of wild plum). H. 69cm.

35. Crocodile mask from Mabuiag, Torres Strait Islands. The British Museum register entry for this piece, which was obtained by Rev. S. McFarlane, has a later annotation by the anthropologist A. C. Haddon, stating that the mask was made especially for McFarlane, at his request, and was never used in a ceremony. It is of astonishing size – about 7ft long. L. c.213cm.

after the Second World War, a European woman living in the Solomons showed local people photographs of African masks, thus starting a new carving tradition. The masks, therefore, seem to be a classic example of tourist art developed specifically for sale to strangers, although a possibility of some tenuous links with old traditional masks cannot be discounted.

In contrast, masking was widespread in the Torres Strait Islands, politically part of Australia but culturally related to the south coast of Papua New Guinea (see figs 33, 34, 35). Masks were used in agricultural ceremonies to promote fertility and celebrate a harvest, in initiations, in funeral rites, in various activities associated with culture heroes, and to ensure a successful fishing expedition or protection against crocodiles. They were made of wood or turtle shell, the latter by far the preferred material in the Torres Strait Islands where it was worked with unparalleled virtuosity. They were worn with leaf skirts or mantles and were of two main types: those representing a human face, of wood or turtle shell, and large composite animal masks, made mainly of turtle shell.

The finest human face masks in wood come from Saibai, those in turtle shell from Mer and Erub.

Animal masks, some of them of great complexity and considerable size, are particularly characteristic of the western islands and represent sea creatures. The whole body of the animal can be represented or just the head; in some a human face is added.

NEW GUINEA

The Papuan Gulf region of Papua New Guinea, north of the Strait, is also noted for its masks. Traditionally the Gulf people were organised into totemic clans and had no hereditary chiefs, the older men possessing the power and influence. Rich ceremonial life was centred on large men's houses and expressed itself in prolonged dramatic rituals for which a great number of ceremonial objects, including masks, were created. Ceremonies consisted of a series of activities and a full cycle could take many years to complete. The purpose of the ceremonies varied among different groups:

it could be promotion of garden fertility, initiation of boys and girls into adult sex life, strengthening of the participants and prevention of sickness or initiation into various cults. The Elema tribe, living west of the Orokolo Bay in the Gulf, performed two ceremonial cycles: one dedicated to the bush spirits, the other to the sea spirits. They were known among the western Elema respectively as *Kovave* and *Hevehe* (see fig. 36).

It is worth looking in some detail at the latter, which was studied and described by anthropologist F. E. Williams and further analysed by C. J. Mamiya and E. C. Sumnik, in order to illustrate the significance of the masquerade.

Hevehe was a cycle of ceremonies during which the dangerous female sea spirits, *ma-hevehe*, were believed to visit the village periodically, bringing to the men's house, or the *eravo*, various materials for the construction of masks. Hevehe masks represented the spirits' daughters, who presented themselves to the assembled crowds at the climax of the cycle. The masks, large vertical ovals with a framework of cane, wood and basketry, covered with ornamented barkcloth, their lower part in the form of a human face, were worn with a long mantle of sago leaves. The decision to begin the Hevehe was made by members of the eravo and its elders. As the ceremony required a great deal of labour (the masks were over 2m high and Williams mentions 120 masks appearing in one particular ceremony) and the accumulation of food, pigs and shell ornaments (for gift presentations punctuating various stages of the cycle), it was embarked upon only in times of plenty. A full Hevehe cycle could take ten to twenty years to complete.

The first major ceremony of the cycle, *Hevehe Karawa*, initiated young men into the secret of the spirits: the youths were ambushed on the beach by men carrying the cane bent into mask shapes and impersonating the spirits. Then the construction of the masks began. This proceeded in eleven stages, each introduced by the Hevehe Karawa ceremony at which the 'spirits' brought additional materials for the masks. When a new door for the eravo was made (the eravo had a very high gable to admit the huge masks), there was an interlude during which masks of a different type appeared. Called *eharo*, they were also made of barkcloth, but were much smaller, conical or round, often surmounted by totemic emblems (see fig. 37).

When the Hevehe masks had been finished, boys were initiated into the secrets of the masks: they tried them on and learned to move while wearing them. The climax came just before sunrise when the eravo doors were opened and the masks appeared. Williams described 'this supreme moment when the hevehe, after wellnigh twenty years of confinement, issue forth to commence the brief fulfilment of their existence. In the grey light of early morning the first of them, "Koraia", stood framed against the blackness of the open door – a tall, fantastic figure, silvery white, its coloured patterns

36. Mask from the Gulf Province, Papua New Guinea. Made of barkcloth, with painted designs outlined with strips of cane, and a leaf skirt, such masks were used in the ceremonial cycle, dedicated to the bush spirits, called *Kovave* among the Elema people. At the conclusion of the cycle the masks were burned. H. 154cm.

37. *Eharo* mask, Elema, Gulf Province, Papua New Guinea. Made of barkcloth, with a design formed of thin cane strips stitched to the cloth, filled with pigment. Such masks, some representing mythological characters, others individual improvisations, were used to re-enact mythological events and in dances, providing entertainment and imparting a carnival atmosphere during one stage of the *Hevehe* cycle. H. 49.5cm.

in the atmosphere of dawn appearing pale and very delicate . . . A strange, other-worldly figure, and a heathenish one, no doubt; but none who saw it poised on that dark threshold could have failed to call it beautiful'. Carrying drums, and to the accompaniment of more drums, the masked men moved to the beach where they danced. For a month they danced every day until finally the cycle was concluded with yet another feast and the ritual shooting of the masks with arrows, after which they were burned.

The Hevehe ceremony can be interpreted on several different levels. Seen through the initiates' eyes, it could be described as a process of dis-illusionment. As boys, they discover that the masks are not the spirits' daughters but men disguised; and later, as young adults, that the great noise the spirits make when they come from the sea is made by men pretending to be spirits. The secrets revealed, there is no longer a mystery.

At the same time the process of initiation is a means of social advance-ment. Acquisition of knowledge brings with it power for it is the older men, who know how to make masks, who orchestrate the ceremonial cycle, and to whom the largest share of repeated presentations and exchanges of food and valuables accrues. The ceremony reinforces the privileged pos-ition of the older men, on whose knowledge it depends for its success.

On the economic level, the conclusion of each stage of the cycle triggers the intensification of food production without which the continuation of the ceremony would be impossible. Food production – pig-rearing in par-ticular – involves women whose role is ambivalent and typical of their function in a Melanesian masquerade. On the one hand, they are excluded from the Hevehe secrets; on the other, they produce the material from which the masks' mantles are made and their cooperation is needed both in food production and audience participation. Although the Hevehe, being an exclusively male cult, withholds from them the powers it imparts to its members, it also recognises their contribution: at one stage there is a special gift presentation between women, albeit a symbolic one, for the gifts have been provided by men who fulfil in this way some of their own varied and complex gift obligations and enhance their own prestige.

Masks similar to those of the Elema are found among other groups in the Gulf although the ceremonial context in which they appear differs. Barkcloth masks predominate in the eastern half of the Gulf; in the west masks are made of basketry, but all of them are based on the motif of the human face.

Among the Gogodala who live inland on the Aramia River, in the extreme west of the Gulf area, and who have their own, very distinctive style, masks are made of light wood in the form of an oval plaque, painted with elegant curvilinear decoration in black, red, yellow and white. One type, 1 to 2m high, has a totemic design with a central motive or the 'eye' of shell surrounded with red abrus seeds and a crescent-shaped aperture at

the lower end to look through. The other type represents a human face, that of a clan ancestor. These masks, with a ceremonial dress of sago fronds, feather plumes and plaited bands, were worn at initiation ceremonies. After a period of missionary-induced almost total decline, the tradition of mask-making was revived as part of the successful cultural renaissance which the Gogodala went through in the 1970s.

Although masks are characteristic of the eastern half of the island of New Guinea and of the greater part of the neighbouring Bismarck Archipelago (now all forming the independent state of Papua New Guinea), they are rare in the western half (now Irian Jaya, a province of Indonesia). Among the Asmat people of the south coast, who used to be head- hunters with a highly developed ancestor cult, the masks appear in ceremonies commemorating the recently dead, during which the mask-wearers impersonate their dead kinsmen. There are two types of masks. The first is a mask combined with a bodice, made of fine vegetable-fibre string and covering the head and the upper torso, worn with sago-frond skirt and sleeves (see fig. 38). The other is much simpler, consisting of a basketry cone with small peep-holes and is also worn with a skirt.

When the masks are completed, they are named, and as the spirits of the ancestors they appear for the last time before their kinsmen. The conical mask plays an ambivalent role for, while representing an ancestor, it is also a clownish figure, with connotations of fertility. At the conclusion of the ceremony the masks are chased into the men's house whence they depart into the world of the dead.

The masquerade stresses the continuity of life in spite of death, both through the fertility associations of the conical mask, and through the identification of the living with the dead. This identification is more than symbolic, for the men wearing the masks adopt the children of the dead kinsmen whom they impersonate.

Masks similar to the Asmat bodice masks are found also among the Mimika, the Asmat's neighbours to the west, where, as Kooijman has noted, they are also associated with the dead and the continuation of life.

On mainland Papua New Guinea the Sepik River region is an area of astonishing cultural variety. Its artistic diversity and richness are unique in Oceania, and it is probably one of the most inventive and prolific art centres in the world. This artistic wealth is evident in the wide range of ceremonial objects, ornamentation of utilitarian artefacts, the forms, the media and the techniques employed. Masks are a case in point. Made usually of wood or basketry, in different forms and sizes, they are decorated with a bewildering variety of ornaments: shells, beads, feathers, teeth, tusks, seeds, and various vegetable fibres (see fig. 39). The majority are also painted, usually in white, black, red, yellow and grey. Masks, representing mythological beings, spirits or the dead, were – and in some areas still are

38. Mask from the Asmat area, Irian Jaya. Collected in 1961 in Momogo, Upper Pomatsj River, it has a painted bodice of vegetable-fibre string, wood eyes and a decoration of feathers and coix seeds. The sleeves and skirt are of sago fronds. H. 188cm.

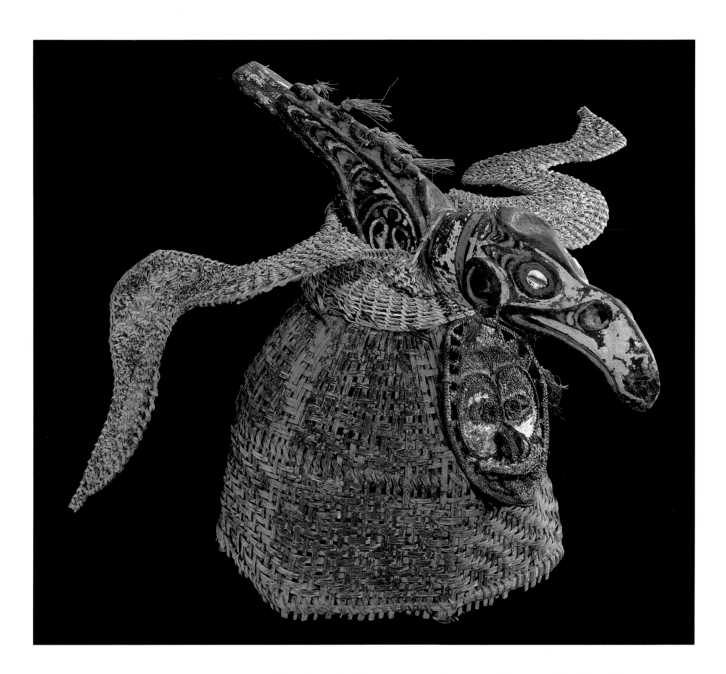

39. Basketry mask, Sepik River, Papua New Guinea. Ornamented with pigment, it is surmounted by a carved and painted wooden bird with eyes of small cowrie shells. H. 45cm.

– used in the whole spectrum of ceremonies associated with initiations, mourning rites and the agricultural cycle.

Wood masks from the Sepik are usually oval, with special emphasis on the nose: in some it is thick and bulbous, in others it is pointed and greatly elongated, sometimes joining the chin (see fig. 41). Basketry masks often have similarly elongated noses. A great variety of basketry masks is made among the Abelam people living north of the middle course of the Sepik, most for the decoration of huge ceremonial yams, grown competitively by men, but some are worn (see fig. 40).

Masks, as representations of the human face, are a ubiquitous phenomenon in Sepik material culture. They appear in all sizes, from huge masks

40. Basketry mask from the Wosera sub-district of the Abelam area, East Sepik Province, Papua New Guinea. A great variety of basketry masks are made by the Abelam, most of them for decorating large ceremonial yams, but helmet masks, such as this, are worn, with a full-length leaf mantle and a necklace of bright red fruit. H. 42cm.

on house gables to tiny amulets; they decorate ceremonial houses, implements and costumes and they are carried as good-luck charms on hunting or fishing expeditions. Only a proportion of them are worn.

Mask-making is a thriving art in Papua New Guinea, often serving the tourist industry. Styles and sizes are often adjusted to suit the taste of customers, forms are simplified to save the carver's time, or elaborated to the point of the bizarre in order to intrigue or shock the customer. Many such souvenirs bear only a vague resemblance to the sophisticated traditional masks, but some craftsmen take great pride in maintaining high standards and producing pieces of good quality, and experimentation in their hands may lead to interesting results.

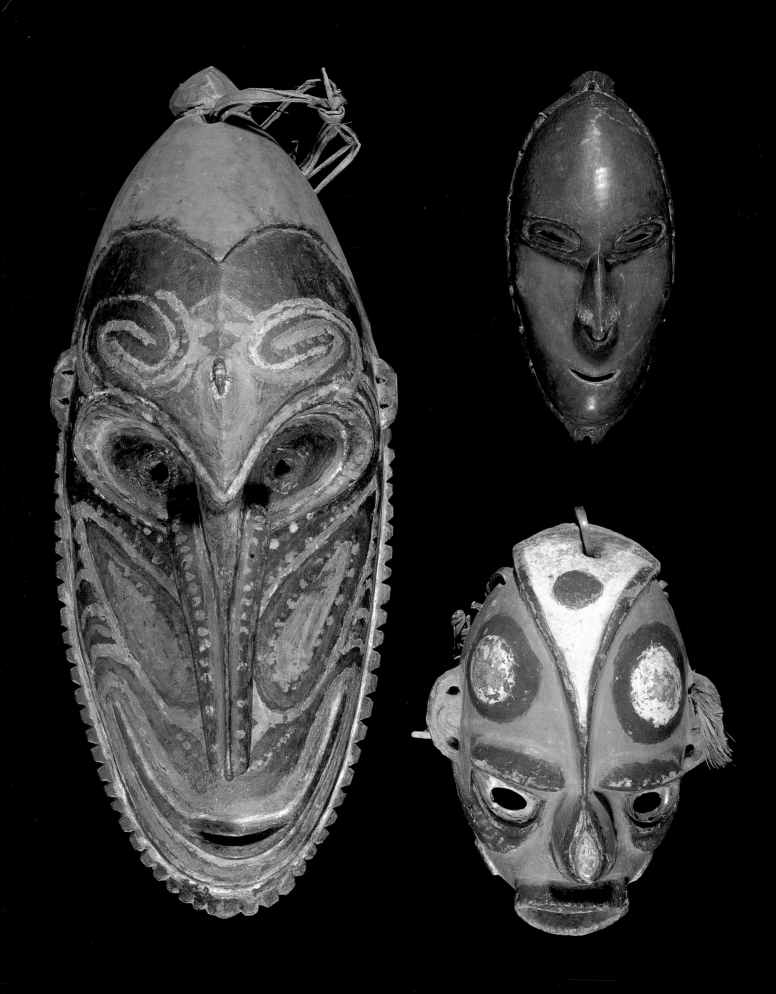

Masks of a fairly uniform style are characteristic of the Astrolabe Bay and the Huon Gulf region of northeastern Papua New Guinea, including the islands of Vitiaz Strait, which separates the mainland from New Britain, and the westernmost part of New Britain itself. Ceremonial life of this area was dominated by the secret cult called *Balum*, centred on the spirit of the same name and involving the initiation of boys, performed in a specially-built house in the bush.

Masks used in the context of the cult on Tami Islands (and other islands of the Vitiaz Strait) and representing the cult spirit known there as *Kani*, are oblong and painted white with black and red decoration. The Tami islanders also had masks made of barkcloth, associated with *Tago* spirits, which belonged to individual family groups. Worn during ceremonies re-enacting the arrival and departure of the spirits, the masks are oval with a round cap-like head covering, the face painted in a manner similar to that of the wood mask (see fig. 42).

Wood masks of the Kilenge people of the western tip of New Britain are very similar in style to those of the Tami Islanders. Masks from the

Astrolabe Bay, with their protruding eyes and large curved noses, and the painted cylindrical helmet masks from the Witu Islands off west New Britain, although different, still somehow show an affinity with the formal-ity of style and the brooding quality of the Huon-style masks. In addition, the Kilenge people have masks/headdresses (the Kilenge themselves do not make a distinction between masks and headdresses, seeing them all

as different versions of decorative headpieces) made of coconut spathe, painted and decorated with feathers and various vegetable fibres, which are used in cyclical ceremonial dances called *narogo*. Interestingly, the success of such ceremonial cycles is evaluated not so much in terms of presentation as essentially in terms of sufficiency of food provided for the participants and the spectators and the numbers of pigs exchanged, thus, as Zelenietz and Grant have noted, revealing once again the socio-economic matrix of the ceremony.

BISMARCK ARCHIPELAGO

In the Bismarck Archipelago provinces of Papua New Guinea masks are found in abundance in New Ireland and New Britain.

In New Ireland masks are used in the context of complex and elaborate mortuary ceremonies called *Malanggan*, for which a great number of carvings and masks (also known by their generic term as *malanggan*) are made and which are the most important element of New Ireland culture. As so often in Melanesia, the ceremony involves a great deal of expense – feasting and payments, inextricably connected with it, necessitate accumulation of food and shell money – so it is performed months or even years after death and for several dead simultaneously.

Malanggan objects are owned, not in the sense of physical ownership of a carving, but in the sense of copyright to the form and style of the pieces and accompanying rites. Such ownership can be bought, upon which the original owner loses the right to use that particular malanggan in future. Malanggans are, therefore, acquired in order to replace those sold, and as a matter of prestige since the splendour of the malanggan display testifies to the honour and material resources of its sponsors (see fig. 30).

In this sense the Malanggan not only bids farewell to the dead but also demonstrates the vitality of the living who are able to put on a such a prestigious display. As in other ceremonies described above, Malanggan is a communal effort, in which deals are made and obligations undertaken, to be fulfilled in another Malanggan ceremony in the years to come.

Similar displays are also made for initiation ceremonies and there is a parallel here: as the dead are transferred to the world of the spirits, so the boys are transferred from the world of women and children to that of adult men. The dead members of the community are replaced by the newly-fledged adults. As among the Asmat, the continuity of life is maintained and the community revitalised.

In Malanggan displays pride of place is given to carvings of various types, but masks play an important role, too (see fig. 43). All the malanggan objects bear the hallmark of the same general and unmistakable style characterised by sculptural intricacy and complexity, polychrome surface ornamentation and the use of snail operculae for eyes. The masks are

43. Intricately carved and complex *malanggan* mask, New Ireland, Papua New Guinea. Malanggan masks can represent dead ancestors, the spiritual double of an individual known as *ges*, or various bush spirits. Collected by Romilly, and from the same malanggan house as the helmet mask (fig. 30). H. 61cm.

45. Contemporary Baining mask, East New Britain, Papua New Guinea. Made of barkcloth covering a cane frame and painted, masks of this type, used in night dances, are widespread among the Baining. They represent animals or plants, the whole object or a distinctive feature, such as the beak of a hornbill; to European eyes, however, the thing represented is not always instantly recognisable. H. 124cm.

44. Tolai mask, East New Britain, Papua New Guinea. It is carved from soft wood and painted. The red round the chin and on the hat is European cloth. The double-bodied snake finial is also of wood, partly painted white and green, partly covered with white-spotted European cloth. Collected by Rev. George Brown, a missionary, between 1875 and 1881. H. 76cm.

extremely varied, some are designed to be worn, others to be displayed; some are kept to be used repeatedly, others are destroyed after the ceremony with the rest of the display.

Today the Malanggan tradition continues but in a changed and reduced form. Under the influence of Christianity, as Lewis points out, malanggan carvings have been largely displaced by cement grave markers called *smel*, and those which are still made are often simplified and more roughly executed than in the past.

In New Britain masks are particularly important among the Tolai (see fig. 44), Baining and Sulka peoples of Gazelle Peninsula of the eastern half of the island.

Among the Tolai and the related Duke of York Islanders, tall conical masks worn with leaf mantles are associated with secret societies into which men are inititated through payments of the all-important shell currency of the area. An example from Karavar, a small Duke of York island, illustrates well the social importance of such societies called here *Dukduk*.

There are two types of masks: the female *tubuan*, by far the most important, whose characteristic feature is large painted eyes of concentric circles; and the male *dukduk* which, although decorated, does not have eyes. Purchasing the copyright to a particular form of dukduk is expensive but as such purchases are made on the basis of reciprocity, nearly all adult men have their own dukduks. The acquisition of the tubuan, however, to which many aspire but few achieve, is more demanding but it opens a possibility of influence and power. Only a tubuan owner can sponsor the mortuary ceremony through which prestige is achieved, and tubuan owners pass judgements in the ritual court, collecting the lion's share of the fines imposed. The masks here are external symbols of the graded system which imposes order on the society.

The Baining area is notable for its spectacular, inventive and rather surreal barkcloth masks. The most impressive are enormous *hareiga* masks, some of them up to 12m high, which were worn at daytime ceremonies commemorating the dead and celebrating the taro harvest. Such masks have a long narrow tubular body and a large elongated, rounded or pointed head with small ears; at the upper part of the body and at the bottom are small spindly extensions representing limbs. These masks, from the northwest Baining, are no longer made, although different types of tall daytime masks are still produced and used. Smaller, more varied masks are associated with night dances and boys' initiations (see fig. 45).

The tradition of the masked dances has survived among the Baining and the barkcloth masks are still made, often for performances put on for tourists or visiting dignitaries.

The most colourful of New Britain masks are those of the Sulka people. They are made from parallel narrow strips of pith bound around a cone-

46. Old Sulka mask, East New Britain, Papua New Guinea. It is made entirely of vegetable materials: the wood and cane frame is covered with narrow strips of pith, which are painted. The fringe is of leaves and vegetable fibre decorates the top of the mask. H. 63cm.

shaped framework. A particularly impressive type of mask consists of a base cone surmounted by a large, sometimes huge, umbrella-like disc, the underside of which is ornamented with painted designs. The masks have additional decoration of feathers and are worn with leaf skirts.

Traditionally the masks were connected with boys' initiations and with mortuary ceremonies (see fig. 46). Representing spirits, the masks were dangerous and were burned after the ceremony at which they appeared. Women and children were allowed to see the masks only on the occasion of their public performance. Otherwise anything connected with the masks – the method of manufacture, the materials, the final destruction – was concealed from them with the utmost secrecy.

47. Contemporary Sulka mask, East New Britain, Papua New Guinea. Traditional in form, it is also innovative: the cone base is made from hardened base of palm leaf and it is decorated with glossy European paint. It was made by Paul Anis from Kilalum, and was used during an ordination ceremony in 1982. H. 112cm.

These attitudes still persist and masks are still made, although they are now used in different contexts (see fig. 47). In 1982, at Guma Catholic Mission at Wide Bay, masked dancers participated in festivities celebrating the ordination of a local priest and a masked figure accompanied the ordin- and to the altar, an interesting example of the integration of old customs into the new reality (Hill, 1982).

Polynesia and Micronesia

In Polynesia and Micronesia masks are extremely rare. In fact, in Polynesia there is no reliable evidence for the existence of masks before the arrival of Europeans, except for the so-called mourner's costume in Tahiti (see fig.

48). The costume, and the ceremony at which it appeared, were described in various accounts of Captain Cook's voyages, and a number of such dresses were collected on the second and third voyages (1772–5 and 1776–80). Made of barkcloth and feathers, with a face mask of pearl shells, it was worn during a funeral ceremony by the chief mourner. The question of whether the dress was a true mask, or simply a special type of costume, remains unresolved.

Evidence for mask-like objects in Hawaii comes from the same early period: drawings by Webber, the artist on Cook's third voyage, show rowers of a Hawaiian canoe wearing gourd helmets partly covering the face. Lieutenant King, who accompanied Cook, wrote that the purpose of the helmets eluded the English: 'Whether they may not likewise be used as a defence for the head against stones, for which they seem best designed, or in some of their public games, or be merely intended for the purpose of mummery, we could never inform ourselves'. Within the context of Hawaiian culture one is more inclined to think of them as ceremonial helmets with 'visors' rather than masks, but their precise significance remains uncertain.

Records of the only other masks in Polynesia – made of barkcloth on Mangaia and of cloth and paper on Easter Island – come from the twentieth century and the masks themselves are almost certainly a post-contact development.

In Fiji, the area often included in Melanesia, but whose culture is much closer to that of Western Polynesia, with which it has maintained contacts for centuries, masks did exist but there are only two extant old examples, collected by the United States Exploring Expedition in 1840. These are simple, plain helmet-type masks of palm spathe, with human hair and beards. Little is known about them, though they have been described and discussed by Clunie and Ligairi. As they appeared in harvest festivals, it is likely that they represented supernatural beings concerned with protection of crops.

In Micronesia masks are found only in the Mortlock group in the Caroline Islands (now Federated States of Micronesia), where they were worn in ceremonies performed to ward off hurricanes and typhoons and to protect the breadfruit crop and appeared also as decoration on the support posts of ceremonial houses (see fig. 4 in Introduction). They are still made today, but for sale to visitors.

There is a record of a shell mask belonging to a local family in Palau (Hidikata, 1973); it was, and presumably still is, used as a talisman to ensure safe childbirth, abundant crops and prosperity, but there is no mention of the mask ever being worn and it may be a late, and certainly idiosyncratic, work of art.

48. Mourner's dress, Society Islands. It is made of barkcloth, with a feather mantle at the back and feather tassels at the sides. Pearl shells form the face mask, surmounted with tropic bird feathers, and decorate the wooden crescent breast ornament from which is suspended a chest apron of pearl-shell slivers; coconut-shell discs decorate the waist apron. It was presented to Captain Cook during his second voyage. H. 124cm.

FICTIONS AND PARODIES

MASQUERADE IN MEXICO AND HIGHLAND SOUTH AMERICA

'While we are alive, we cannot escape from
masks or names. We are inseparable
from our fictions – our features.'

OCTAVIO PAZ

49. Mezcala style stone mask. Juntas, Rio Frio, State of Guerrero, Mexico,
300 BC–AD 300. These are probably the most simple masks found in
Mesoamerica. It is believed they were used to cover the faces of deceased
members of a ruling elite or important religious figures. H. 17.3cm.

50. Mask maker, Chichihualco, Guerrero, Mexico, 1979. Traditionally, particular families specialised in certain crafts and passed down their knowledge from father to son. In Mexico, mask carvers also make furniture and other domestic wooden items.

51. Gilt copper mask with shell inlays, Moche, Peru, 100 BC–AD 650. The mask, originally coloured red, retains a band of painted snails along the chin. The mask was found in a burial chamber in the Huaca de La Luna at Moche. H. 26cm.

For over 12,000 years the lands from Mexico to South America have cradled and nurtured human cultures. These Latinised lands, streaked with pre-Christian Amerindian beliefs and shreds of African religions carried by the slave trade, have fertilised some of the world's most varied, prolific and enduring traditions of masquerade.

Pre-Hispanic America

The oldest evidence of masks in the Americas is a fossil vertebra of a now extinct llama, from Tequixquiac in Mexico, fashioned sometime between 12,000–10,000 BC to represent the head of a coyote. However, distinct styles of masks, made from sculptured clay and stone, only began to emerge around 1200 BC.

In the Andes, masks were widely used to cover the faces of the dead, whose bodies were carefully dressed and bundled before burial. Some of the earliest masks (c.500 BC), from the Ocucaje region of Peru, were made from dyed red or brown cloth stitched to mummy dressings. Stylised geometrical facial features, sometimes including feline profiles and serpents, proliferated. By Moche times (100 BC–AD 650), burial masks were made from hammered-out sheet gold or copper with nose, teeth and other features separately constructed and soldered on (see figs 51, 52). Chimú (AD 800–1470) masks were made by similar techniques with painted eyes inlaid with turquoise beads. These masks were much simpler and more stylised than their Moche precursors. Many of the Chimú masks in museums today, from tombs in the Lambayeque Valley, were made from gold, silver or copper, some surmounted by an axe-shaped crescent with animals on either side.

Burial masks were less commonly made of clay, although red terracotta masks were made in the Chicama region during an early period (500–250 BC) and later at Pampa Grande (AD 500–700) in northern Peru, while small coarse grey masks dated between AD 1200–1500 were recovered from burials at Portete, Esmeraldas, Ecuador. Pottery masks are also known from the area inhabited by the Tolima in northern Colombia and from the Nariño region in the south of the country.

Andean iconography includes certain ubiquitous characters and motifs that have persisted from Chavín to Inca times (1500 BC–AD 1532). Many early masks and headdresses represented a limited number of animals including the jaguar, puma and fox, some of which assumed increasingly anthropomorphic characteristics among the later Moche and Chimú civilisations. Animal masks may have been used during annual religious ceremonies or at initiation and burial rituals to represent the intervention of ancestral deities. Political divisions of the Inca Empire could be distinguished by the types of mask common to each community or province. The Quechua and Ayamara words for mask, *caynata* or *saynata*, literally

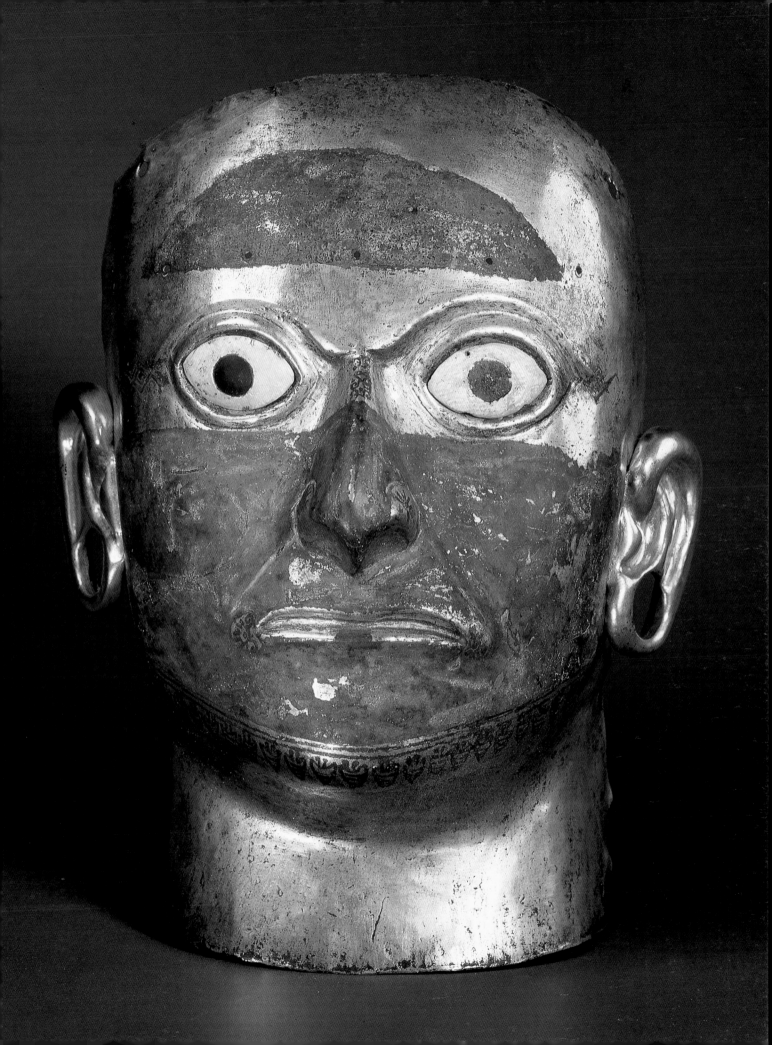

52. Cast gold mask with attached
ear and nose ornaments. Quimbaya
region, Colombia AD 500–1500. The
teeth are shown filed down.
H 12cm.

meant 'masked person' or 'scarecrow', 'to scare children', suggesting a threatening or malevolent association. Masks were also connected with the dead, as suggested by another native descriptive term, *ayachuco* – 'death helmet'.

The Indian chronicler, Guaman Poma de Ayala, illustrated farmers wearing foxes' heads and pelts over their head and shoulders. Masked dance dramas, which incorporated animal characters, were performed during ceremonies dedicated to certain deities. The *llamallama* dance imitated herders who wore animal skins and masks, while the Choquela used vicuña skin costumes.

In Cuzco, Peru, men wearing puma costumes appeared at the end of a ceremony to initiate the sons of noble families into manhood. Jaguar and puma masks were said to represent the animals into which the Inca's ancestors had been transformed – a belief not dissimilar to that in animal companions (*nahuals*) found in Mexico.

In the northern Andes, gold was hammered or cast into mortuary masks for high status burials. A Colombian Quimbaya mask with filed teeth, complete with nose and ear ornaments, in the British Museum collection, is cast in a strikingly naturalistic style (see fig. 52).

The earliest undisputed evidence of masquerade in Mesoamerica dates to the middle pre-classic period (1000–300 BC). Here can be found two clearly defined traditions: the pre-classic village cultures centred on the valley of Mexico and the Olmec civilisation dispersed across the states of Veracruz, Tabasco, Puebla, Morelos and Guerrero. Ceramic masks from the late pre-classic period (300 BC–AD 300) have also been retrieved from the west Mexican states of Colima, Jalisco and Nayarit and from Chupicuaro in Guanajuato. The largest number of masks from this period have been found at Tlatilco, Xochipala and Tlapacoya in the valley of Mexico, and at the Olmec sites of Arrollo Pesquero, San Lorenzo and Tenenexpan. Outside the Valley of Mexico and the Olmec areas, isolated regional styles proliferated and, in some areas at least, body painting may have been more widespread than masquerade. Many of the ceramic masks from the Valley of Mexico share similar iconographic features to those associated with gods during later periods of Mexican history. The rounded, smooth, expressionless faces with circular eyes and open mouths from Tlatilco, may have represented the skin masks associated with the god Xipe Totec which the Aztec used in the spring festivals for agricultural renewal. Another type of mask, with grotesque features, deep sunken eyes and wrinkled skin, could be related to the fire god, who later assumed the name of Huehueteotl, while others, with feline characteristics and crocodilian teeth, may have been a version of the Olmec were-jaguar or dragon. Fundamental Mesoamerican categories such as 'duality' were already expressed in masks and figurines of the period. Masks representing half a living face and half

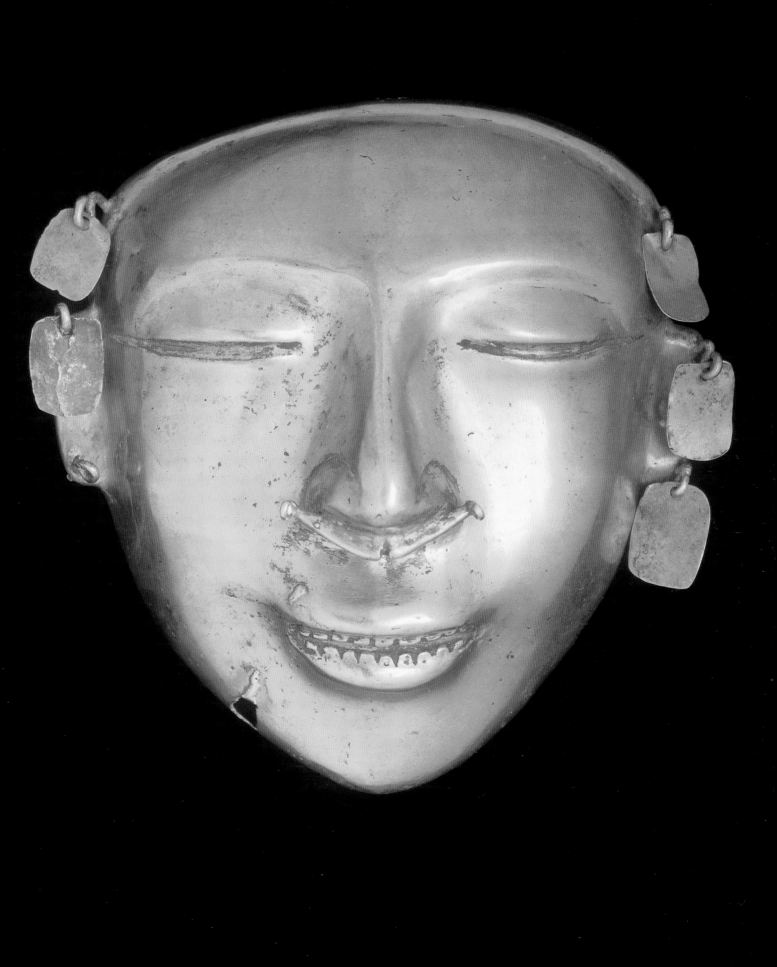

53. Stone mask, Teotihuacan, State of Mexico, Mexico. Like fig. 5, this is a highly stylised mask showing the influence of the Mezcala style from north-east Guerrero, AD 300–650. H. 22cm.

54. Olmec-style mask of greenish jade, recently repaired and restored. The engraving has been refilled with cinnabar. Arroyo Pesquero (?), Veracruz, Mexico, 900–600 BC. H. 16.5cm.

a fleshless skull, or half man and half animal, have been found at various sites in central Mexico. An extraordinary ceramic head from this region shows a skull cut down the centre to reveal the features of old age, which itself opens to show a youthful face underneath. This suggests the complex view of a multi-levelled reality which may have influenced pre-classic ideas underlying the nature and uses of masks.

The Olmec, unlike their central Mexican neighbours, used jade, serpentine, fuchsite, quartzite or onyx in the production of masks. Human images outnumber deities, but masks also represented the Olmec dragon, the Bird Monster and the ubiquitous were-jaguar. On more naturalistic masks, such as those from Arrollo Pesquero, Veracruz, profiles of deities were carved and outlined in cinnabar (see fig. 53). Similarly, the sculpture of the so-called Lord of Las Limas is decorated by six partially-masked figures who are believed to represent the principal deities of the Olmec pantheon. Other figures representing ball players and acrobats sometimes wear mouth masks which leave the upper part of the face uncovered.

In Olmec art, human identity is rarely submerged by the animal or deity represented by the mask. A mural at Oxtotitlan, Guerrero, showing a seated figure wearing the full costume and mask of the Bird Monster, is drawn in X-ray style to reveal the human identity of its wearer. Olmec rulers, such as those shown on stela 3 at La Venta and petroglyph 1 at Chalcatzingo, wear elaborate headdresses probably intended to make a supernatural association without negating the identity of the wearer.

A third distinct stylistic tradition of masks in Mesoamerica had its origin in the late pre-classic period around the Mezcala and Chontal regions of north-east Guerrero (see fig. 49). These flattened masks with minimal features are usually perforated in the centre of the forehead for suspension and may have been used to cover the faces of the dead. The Mezcala style, devoid of all the expressive qualities of central Mexican or Olmec masks, appears to have exerted a strong influence on the later angular and accentuated trapezoidal style of stone masks associated with the great metropolitan centre of Teotihuacan (AD 300–650). Many of the surviving stone masks have no openings for eyes – some are encrusted with turquoise and coral mosaics or have inlays of obsidian pyrite or mother of pearl around their eyes and teeth (see fig. 5 in Introduction). Even though none of the Teotihuacan masks have been found in-situ, like their Mezcala counterparts, it is generally assumed that they were intended for funerary use.

As is repeatedly found throughout Mesoamerica, murals and vase paintings illustrate a rich variety of masquerades, which differ considerably from surviving masks. The murals in the palaces of Tepantitla and Tetitla at Teotihuacan illustrate either gods or masked priests wearing elaborate feather headdresses, mounted over masks probably made of wood (see fig. 56, *left*). In the Maya country, the Bonampak murals show a more vigorous

56. (*above left*) Mural painting of a Water Goddess. Tepantitla Palace, Teotihuacan, State of Mexico, Mexico, AD 300–450. The goddess wears an ornate feather headdress with an owl-like mask and richly decorated costume. Water, symbol of fertility and abundance, drips from her fingers and from the branches of the tree behind her. She is attended by two acolytes. The scene has often been identified with accounts of Tlalocan, the Aztec aquatic paradise reserved for those who had died by drowning.

(*above right*) Mural painting of musicians and entertainers. Room 1, Structure 1, Bonampak, State of Chiapas, Mexico, AD 790–2. Among the elaborate masks of the entertainers, crustacean and crocodile headdresses can be identified. These masks do not, however, correspond to the iconography of known Maya supernaturals and their meaning is elusive.

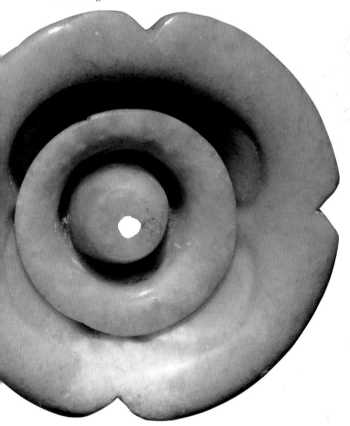

55. Mosaic mask in jade, obsidian and shell. Maya, AD 250–900. The large earspools identify the mask as representing an important lord. H. 15cm.

57. Jade mosaic mask with eyes and mouth inlaid with shell and pyrite. Maya, Tikal, Guatemala, AD 527. This portrait mask was found in a high-status burial chamber and probably represents the deceased with whom it was interned. H. 33cm.

scene of masked entertainers and musicians, whose masks have no surviving counterparts (see fig. 56, *right*).

The Maya, in southern Mexico, Guatemala and Honduras, used a more naturalistic style of portraiture for funerary masks (see figs 54, 57). An exceptional jade mosaic portrait of Pacal, who acceded to the throne at Palenque in AD 615 and ruled until 683, was found in the burial chamber under the Temple of the Inscriptions. Most of the surviving Maya masks also have funerary or underworld associations, such as the British Museum's mask-like stone head representing the underworld God Gl of the Palenque Triad. Jade masquettes and larger carvings, such as the portrait head from Tambla near Comayaqua, Honduras, also in the British

Museum, formed part of elaborate pendants, pectorals and belts worn for ceremonial occasions by Mayan kings and members of the elite.

With the exception of a few masks made of beaten gold from the sacred well at Chichen-Itza, and a copper masquette now in the British Museum, believed to represent the merchant god Ek Chuah, metal masks are rare.

The Aztec codices and the sixteenth-century Spanish accounts of late post-classic civilisations (AD 1200–1519), provide a rich (if sometimes enigmatic) source of information about the use and significance of masks in Mesoamerica. The *Codex Mendoza* and the *Matrícula de Tributos* list the towns that provided precious stones, feathers, animal pelts and sometimes masks themselves – objects that were paid as tribute to the centralised Aztec state. Ten turquoise masks were exacted as part of the annual tribute demanded from the town of Yohualtepec in Oaxaca. Other towns in the Veracruz, Oaxaca and Puebla regions supplied precious stones as tribute to the Aztec state, which were used by Mixtec craftsmen in making mosaic masks.

Five distinct but related uses of masks can be discerned in late post-classic Mexico.

FUNERARY USES

The Aztec wrapped the bodies of high-ranking priests and rulers in fine fabrics and placed masks over their faces before they were cremated. After cremation, secondary bundles were made representing the deceased, re-dressed in still finer clothes and wearing more elaborate masks. Burial masks appear to have represented the deities with whom the ruler was most closely affiliated. According to the Franciscan priest and chronicler Fr Diego Durán, the secondary images of the deceased emperor Axayacatl (1469–81), and his successor Tizoc (1481–6), had five layers of costume, complete with masks. The first represented the king himself, while successive masks represented Huitzilopochtli (the state patron), Tlaloc (the rain god and founder of the royal house), Xipe Totec (the god associated with spring and renewal, also identified with the privilege of exacting tribute), and Quetzalcoatl-Ehecatl (the wind god and founder of the Aztec nobility). Such images clearly combined supernatural qualities with politically inspired attributes that commemorated and legitimated the system of theocratic rulership (see figs 60, 61).

IMPERSONATION OF DEITIES

Codices more commonly picture masked deities or their priestly impersonators. In many depictions, divinities or priests are illustrated with their characteristic face paint, body decoration and headdresses, but Tlaloc, Quetzalcoatl-Ehecatl and the underworld god Mictlantecuhtli are frequently shown masked. Folio 29r of the *Codex Magliabecchiano* shows a priest carrying an ear of corn in one hand and a well-hewn Tlaloc mask in

58. (*overleaf*) Stone mask of Xipe Totec, Aztec, AD 1200–1519. The low relief carving on the inside shows the god dressed in his typical conical headdress and wearing a flayed skin. He carries a rattle stick, the symbol of agricultural fertility, and a human skull. The mask still bears traces of red pigment, a colour closely associated with Xipe Totec. H. 22.8cm.

59. Mosaic covered skull, believed to represent the God Tezcatlipoca. Mixtec/Aztec, AD 1200–1519. The skull may have belonged to an important man-god closely identified with Tezcatlipoca. Subsequent mosaic decoration would have made it an important and perhaps powerful reliquary. H. 20.3cm.

the other, while folios 30r and 55r illustrate jaguar pelts, monkey and avian costumes and headdresses used in ritual fights and religious ceremonies.

TROPHIES

Human skulls and flayed skins were considered prized war trophies and may have provided the most common materials used for masks. Skins were removed from sacrificial victims captured in war and worn during ceremonies such as Tlacaxipehualiztli as tribute paid by the successful warrior to the Aztec state. Although no skin masks have survived, two stone masks in the British Museum and similar ones in Berlin and Vienna depict such masks, showing the skin tightly drawn over the face with slits for the eyes and mouth (see fig. 58).

Skull masks, usually undecorated and used as tribute, were also not uncommon. Exceptional skull masks such as that in the British Museum decorated with alternate bands of turquoise and lignite, a turquoise-encrusted skull from Teotitlan del Camino, Oaxaca (National Museum of Ethnography, Leiden) and the elaborately carved skull from the Maya site of Kaminaljuyu near present-day Guatemala City, may have been important reliquaries closely associated with divine power (see fig. 59).

WARRIOR HEADDRESSES

Numerous sculptures, illustrations and friezes show a further use of masks by warriors. The two principal military orders – Eagle and Jaguar knights – wore pelts and costumes with realistic animal headdresses, representing the animal with which they identified (see fig. 62). These costumes, masterfully painted in the murals at Cacaxtla, State of Tlaxcala, continued to be depicted after the Conquest in documents such as the History of Tlaxcala and in indigenous wall paintings like those in the convents of Ixmiquilpan and Tlayacapan.

ENTERTAINMENT

Masks were also used by court entertainers impersonating animals and neighbouring peoples (who were despised by the Aztec). While it has been argued that such farces were encouraged because they reiterated the feats of Aztec conquests and the subordinate role of conquered peoples, the performers included deformed and retarded actors thought by the Aztec to have been favoured by the gods. Such entertainments, therefore, perhaps had religious elements closely entwined with their more obvious secular purposes.

Before speculating on the use of masks in late post-classic Mesoamerica, it is necessary to consider the indigenous understanding of what constituted the 'person' and its relationship with wider metaphysical categories. The Aztec notion of the 'person' was not one of a completely independent

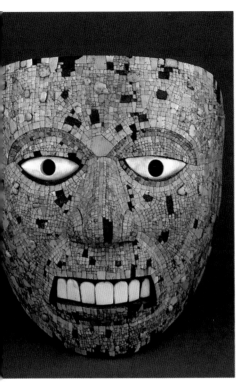

60. (*above*) Mask of turquoise mosaic. Mixtec/Aztec, AD 1200–1519. This mask has been variously identified as representing Quetzalcoatl, the Plumed Serpent, Tonatiuh, the Sun-God, and Tlaltecuhtli, the Earth Monster. Few surviving Aztec masks other than those representing Tlaloc and Xipe Totec are easily identifiable. H. 16.8cm.

61. (*right*) Mask of turquoise mosaic. Mixtec/Aztec, AD 1200–1519. The heads of the serpents encircling the wide circular eyes meet to form the nose. The mask is believed to represent the Rain-God, Tlaloc, the deity most commonly portrayed on turquoise masks. H. 17.8cm.

and freely acting agent whose boundaries corresponded to those of the physical body, as is held in the West. The relationship between the 'person' and animals, plants and natural and supernatural phenomena was neither absolute nor unambiguous.

Personal fate was partly, but not unalterably, conditioned at birth and depended on the sign a child was born under in the 260-day ritual calendar, the Tonalpohualli. Sources disagree as to whether children's names were taken from their day signs or given by their family, but each day sign paired the child with a particular animal, plant or natural phenomenon, with which he or she shared a personal soul. The animal or plant was regarded as an alter ego or patron, whose fate was linked to its human compatriot. Children born on certain days, such as one wind (*ce ehecatl*)

62. Mural painting of a man in a full avian costume including a helmet-like mask enclosing the back and top of the head, wings and talons. Structure A, Cacaxtla, State of Tlaxcala, AD 700–900.

or one rain (*ce quiahuitl*), were thought to have the power to transform themselves into their animal counterpart (*nahual*). This transforming ability was innate, however, and not dependent on masks. It was also believed that certain individuals had particularly powerful 'hearts' (*yollotl*), which gave them uncommon wisdom and abilities. These qualities, thought to have a divine source, made their bodies into receptacles for the numen. Rulers and high-ranking priests were often considered to be closest to this numen and were elevated to an intermediary category between mankind and divinities, thereby permitting their offices to be legitimated by divine association.

Aztec masquerade, therefore, does not appear to have been either a means of achieving effacement or transformation. The circumstances under which masks were worn or exhibited – funerary bundles, deity impersonators, warriors, court entertainers, during ceremonies or displayed as tribute – combined religious and political significance. Pictorial conventions of representing masked persons that enable both the natural face and mask to be seen, the use of mouth masks, and the greater popularity of headdresses and face paint, suggest they were meant to allude to the co-existence of multiple human, natural and supernatural qualities within the same body. This interpretation is borne out by the indigenous term for mask, *xayacatl*, meaning 'face', which was considered to be the external expression of a person's heart.

Masks were also thought to possess supernatural power. Folio 34 of the *Codex Borbonicus* shows how, during the New Fire Ceremony, women and children were locked in their homes and protected by masks to prevent malevolent spirits transforming them into animals. This is one of few examples where effacement was clearly intended, but rather than transforming their wearers, the masks safeguarded their human identity. Masks were thought also to have curative powers and were placed over the head of an ailing emperor to aid recovery. Furthermore, the Jaguar and Eagle costumes were probably meant to allude to the ferocity, agility and bravery of the animals with which their wearers identified and with whom, they believed, they shared a personal soul.

The power attributed to masks probably grew out of their close association with the numen. Skulls of particularly renowned men-gods, high-ranking military, political or religious officials believed to carry the numen, may have been decorated and preserved as reliquaries. Many of the turquoise mosaic masks recovered from burials in the Mixtec region of Oaxaca and Puebla probably derived their power from previous close associations with the corpses of former men-gods. It has been suggested that the turquoise masks in the British Museum formed part of the regalia of semi-divine priests, and may therefore have been charged with exceptional powers (see figs 60, 61).

Because of the metaphysical power connected with masks, their ownership had strong political implications. The possession of an enemy's skull or skin or the full regalia, including the mask, of a foreign cult signified subjection and the expropriation of a group's supernatural affiliations, effectively leaving them defenceless.

In Mesoamerica, therefore, the primary purpose of masks appears to have been neither to efface nor to reveal, but to serve as vessels or repositories in which the numen was momentarily held, to be placed into contact with the body of the living or deceased. This contact sometimes imparted sufficient spiritual power for masks to be considered reliquaries themselves. Masks symbolised the complex coexistence of 'faces' possible in the human physiognomy.

Colonial and contemporary Latin America

After 1519, first in Mexico and later in Peru, the Spanish systematically purged the indigenous ruling elite and destroyed the theocratic basis of government. Consequently the pre-Columbian traditions of masquerade, connected to authority, warfare, tribute and state-organised ceremonies, were abruptly ended. Nevertheless, certain mask traditions, such as those connected with domestic or community-based ceremonies linked to agriculture and fertility, lingered on. Alarmed by the persistence of indigenous rituals, missionaries, often ambivalently, encouraged Amerindian people to identify some pre-Christian beliefs and rituals with the church-based ceremonies of the Christian calendar. In the Andes, Carnival coincided with the Inca New Year and First Fruits ceremonies. The Feast of the Assumption of the Blessed Virgin (15 August) was celebrated near the time of a pre-Hispanic planting ceremony; the Feast of the Immaculate Conception (8 December) fell close to the ceremony previously dedicated to the Moon, Mamakilla; and All Souls and All Saints (1–2 November) coincided with the period of pre-Hispanic ceremonies for the dead.

This association between ceremonies in the pre-Hispanic and Christian calendars and the conflation of Andean and Mesoamerican deities with Christian saints, provided the basis for new religious traditions that were dramatised in dances and plays. From the eleventh century, Spain had combined Christian-inspired mystery and morality plays with allegorical works to create a new form of liturgical drama, the *auto sacramente*, which proved remarkably open to indigenous ideas and dramatic expressions.

Such dramas were first incorporated into the Corpus Christi celebrations and, despite periodic prohibitions against masquerades in the sixteenth century, were later integrated into the ceremonies marking Christmas, Epiphany, Easter and saints' days. In the Andes, commentators such as Polo de Ondegardo, writing in 1585, acknowledged the similarities between Corpus Christi celebrations, the important Sun ceremony, Intirayami, and a pre-harvest ceremony known as Oncoymitta dedicated to the Pleiades for protection against drought.

In the provinces of Cotopaxi and Tungurahua in Ecuador, where Corpus Christi continues to be lavishly celebrated, the ceremonies open with noisy and acrobatically adept masked devils invading the streets and squares. Other dancers represent angels which, in early Colonial times, were identified with the Andean star gods, previously venerated during the Inca ceremony of Oncoymitta. Dancers wear elaborate costumes consisting of richly embroidered bands hanging from wooden poles balanced across their shoulders, tail apron and breastplate. Complex headdresses supported on a willow frame are decorated with embroidery, coins, mirrors, jewellery and plastic dolls, and surmounted by bunches of feathers. European-style masks are made of painted felt or wire netting with a coin suspended from their nose. The costumes are decorated with a combination of Christian and national icons, linking them to the ceremony in honour of the sacred Eucharist and other Christian images.

Another example of the religious syncretism found throughout the Andes is provided by the Carnival celebrations of the Bolivian city of Oruro. The celebration, primarily in honour of the Virgin of Candelaria, began in 1789 when a certain Fr Montealegre incorporated a dramatisation of the battle between Lucifer and the Archangel Michael to portray the struggle of good over evil and the inevitable victory of Christianity over Andean beliefs. Under the influence of pre-Hispanic and rural beliefs, however, the Virgin of Candelaria became incorporated with Pachamama, the earth, while Lucifer was identified with Supay, a hill spirit or Pachatata, the Earth Lord. Since Pachamama received offerings from farmers in exchange for good harvests, Pachatata also needed to be offered gifts to protect the miners and lead them to rich new veins of metal.

People claim that Pachatata corrupted their traditional lives and values by carrying them away from their rural homes and setting them to work in the mines. The Virgin, however, on behalf of the community, intervened and banished Pachatata into the interior of the earth.

During Carnival this myth is dramatised through the Diablado, a masked dance performance in which Lucifer (Pachatata) and his bands of devils gain temporary sovereignty over the earth until they are pushed back into the mines by the miraculous power of the Virgin of Socovan. Though now more elaborate, until the early twentieth century the costumes of the devil dancers were based on the Spanish and cowboy styles preferred by the rich mine owners, while masks represented the Devil as a horned man (similar to his European image) as was commonly found in other parts of Latin America (see fig. 64). These costumes more clearly expressed how the miners identified the mining economy, their precarious lifestyle and the exploitative mine owners with the immoral universe sanctioned by

63. Monkey masks and costumes, Oruro, Bolivia, 1984. Carnival celebrations incorporate many characters and animals in addition to those directly related to the story of the battle between good and evil. These monkey characters show the strong influence of rural beliefs on Oruro's urban carnival.

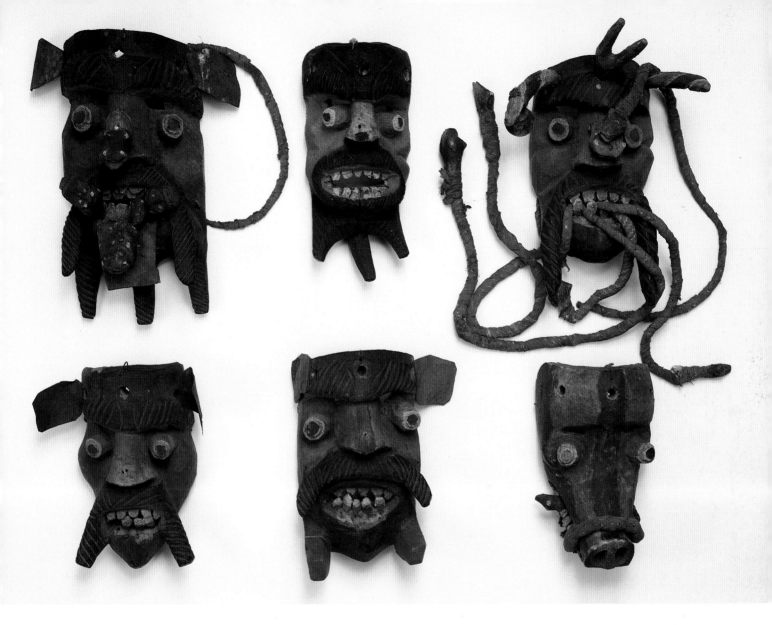

64. Kekchi masks, Aguacate, Belize. Early twentieth century. The masks represent the Devil, his Father, Mother, Wife and two minor Devils who spread lust, dishonesty, drunkenness, hatred, jealousy and death. The Devil commanded the Kekchi to perform the dance regularly in honour of his sovereignty over the world. These masks were collected by Thomas Gann and are now in the British Museum. H. of largest: 46cm.

Lucifer. The defeat of the devil in the Diablado expressed their yearning for an anticipated redemption from hardship and poverty that the Virgin might one day bring about.

Religious festivals are not frozen or static traditions. They have incorporated masquerades influenced by historical events and foreign beliefs. The Morenada dance, also performed during Carnival in Oruro and La Paz, recounts a rebellion by mistreated African slaves working in the mines. Along the central Venezuelan coast, devil dances subsuming African religious elements identify the Zairian origin of former slaves now settled in the region. Finally, the many different dances throughout Mexico and South America dealing with the events of the Conquest, not only express inter-ethnic relations between indigenous communities and Spanish descendants but are an important expression of ethnic identity.

Contemporary masquerade in Mexico and Central America can be divided into three categories. In the first category, the performances are largely derived from the Christian *auto sacramentale*, such as those that treat

65. (*right*) Six masks representing Pedro Alvarado and the Spanish soldiers who conquered the Indian nations of Guatemala. Kekchi, Belize. Early twentieth century. Collected by Thomas Gann. H. of largest 22 cm.

66. (*far right*) Leather helmet masks representing tigers, used in ritual battles during the Festival of the Cross (3 May). Zitlala, State of Guerrero, Mexico. Twentieth century. H. of largest 26.1cm.

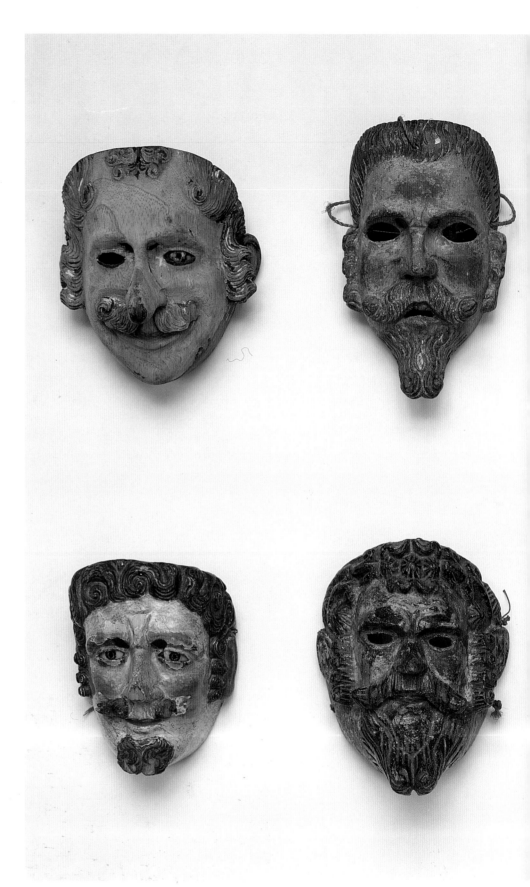

the theme of struggle and conquest, and from morality plays such as the Seven Deadly Sins, the Eight Madmen and the Three Powers. While the organisation and performance of these dances may be little changed since the colonial period, their motivations and meaning may be very different from those originally intended.

The Dance of the Moors and Christians, the most widespread in this category, pits the two sides in mortal combat. The dance drama, based on the fifteenth century re-conquest of the Iberian Peninsula and the expulsion of the Arabs, was presented as an allegory of the battle between Christianity and paganism and the triumph of good over evil. In another version Santiago, the patron saint of the Spaniards credited with innumerable miraculous victories over the various Mesoamerican nations, occupies a more central role and better illustrates the parallels the colonisers attempted to draw between the Re-conquest of the Iberian Peninsula and the Conquest of Mexico.

While the triumph of the Christian Spaniards is usually represented as inevitable, in some dance dramas a millenarian twist, inserted by their indigenous performers, defiantly offers hope of their eventual revindication. Guatemalan combat plays representing the battle between the Quiche Maya, led by Tecum Uman, and the Spaniards under the cruel Pedro de Alvarado, end with the death of the Maya leader and his transformation into a quetzal which flies from the battle ground promising to return and lead his people to eventual victory (see fig. 65).

The second category of Mexican and Central American masquerades incorporate pre-Hispanic and Christian elements. The best documented of these, the Dance of the Tlocololeros, widespread in the states of Guerrero,

68. (*opposite*) Prints of masked wrestlers, Mexico City, 1993. Mexican wrestlers command loyal popular followings. Often bearing names that identify them with legendary heroes of the past, or the comic-book tradition of American superheroes, wrestlers are sometimes romanticised as the embodiment of virtue and ethical values.

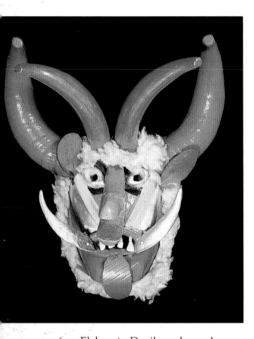

67. Elaborate Devil masks such as these are made for an annual devil mask competition (16 September). The masks characteristically have a proliferation of horns, but vie for the most grotesque features. Teloloápan. State of Guerrero, Mexico. Twentieth century. H. 41.9 cm.

Oaxaca and Morelos, concerns a hunt for a tiger found devastating the fields. The hunters, the Tlocololeros, (who in Chilapa, Guerrero, wear sack-like costumes, wide-brimmed pointed straw hats and wooden masks), have been interpreted as representing rain deities heralding the advent of the wet season, who chase and dispose of the tiger that symbolises the dry season.

In the village of Zitlala, near Chilapa, a ritual battle is enacted during the festival of the Holy Cross (30 April) between protagonists wearing leather helmet masks representing tigers (see fig. 66). The combatants strike each other with thickly tied and knotted lengths of rope until they cause bleeding, intended as an offering for rain.

The third category of masquerades is performed by clowns or buffoons. The Dance of the Old Men, performed in Michoacan, is perhaps related to the Aztec Dance of the Old Hunchbacks, described by Fr Durán. The masks represent near-toothless old men who stagger around supported by walking sticks, causing much hilarity among their audience. Masked clowns often clear dance patios of spectators before the beginning of dances. During the performance they can be found grimacing and taunting the audience and grotesquely mimicking the movements of the dancers.

Masks were previously used in dances performed to fulfil a promise made to the Virgin or to a saint in return for their miraculous intervention, or to request either a communal or a personal favour, for example to bring the rains, to ensure abundant harvests or to protect from or cure illness. They are now just as likely to be made for the external market (see fig. 50). State-sponsored competitions such as those at Teloloápan, in Guerrero, intended to encourage innovations in mask styles (see fig. 67), coupled with demand by collectors for more elaborate masks representing pre-Hispanic themes, stimulated an extraordinary degree of creativity among Mexico's mask-makers during the 1960s, 1970s and 1980s. Some of these new styles have influenced masks used in village ceremonies, but the main trend has been towards secularisation and commercial activity.

In Mexico City, new cults are being established around contemporary real-life masked heroes. In Mexican wrestling matches, where it is common for contestants to be masked, the climax of the game is provided by the victor unmasking his opponent. The most extraordinary figure to have emerged in recent years, however, is Superbarrio, a masked defender of the poor who provides a rallying point against corrupt, inefficient officialdom.

South America generally, and Mexico in particular, continue to pile high different and fragmentary realities, each refracted or concealed behind the mask of others. It is difficult not to wonder just how far removed are a people's aspirations and faith in Superbarrio from beliefs in those more ancient men-gods, which the Spanish spent almost three hundred years in trying to eradicate.

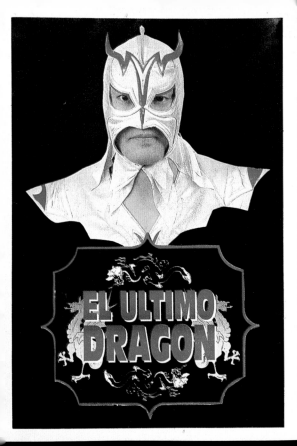

EL ÚLTIMO DRAGÓN

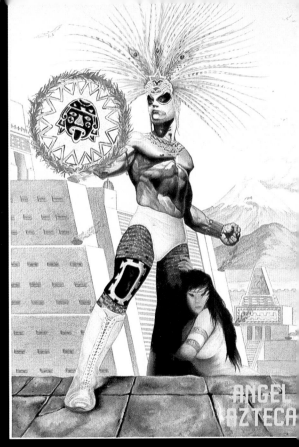

ANGEL AZTECA

SOLAR

EL MISTERIOSO

EL VOLADOR

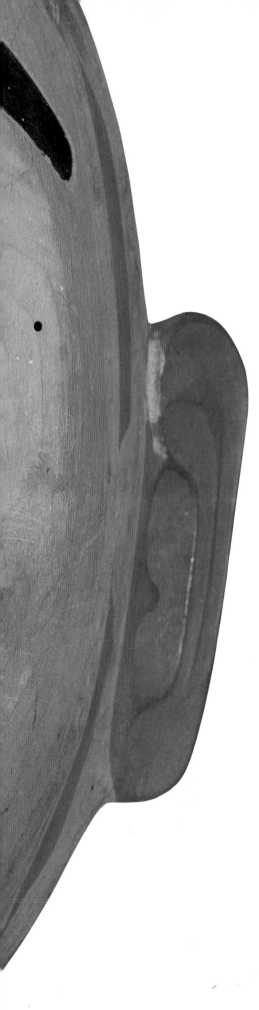

MASKS FROM THE NORTHWEST COAST OF AMERICA

Northwest Coast ceremonialism is often symbolised by the mask – apparently the most easily comprehensible and certainly the most immediate of the artefacts which project Northwest Coast society to the outside world. However, masks are only one small part of the output of highly skilled wood carvers. Most of their work has always been devoted to the pro-

69. Mask of alder possibly representing a specific Haida woman of high birth, wearing a labret and painted with crests of unknown significance. Collected in Hawaii before 1830. H. 23cm.

70. Mask in the form of a bird, probably a Cannibal bird such as Hohokw, from the Kwakwaka'wakw Winter Ceremonial. H. 70cm.

duction of objects such as canoes, houses and boxes, seemingly utilitarian but all possessing symbolic and ritual resonance beyond their functional but elegant forms. More specifically the ceremonial paraphernalia used in feasts (today widely known as potlatches) is highly imaginative: but masks, and masking, are only one aspect of the whole, and not necessarily one endowed with the most meaning. The other articles include much complex paraphernalia, such as intricately-carved rattles, large figures, poles, screens and puppets, as well as masks. Conversely, many apparently insignificant raw materials, such as red cedar bark and eagle down, of central ceremonial importance, may be used in ritual, although cedar bark may also be very carefully woven into, for instance, headrings. Meaning, and the communication of meaning, may derive from apparently prosaic materials and ordinary actions, yet outsiders may still perceive the mask as the central feature of ceremonialism. This is best indicated by the occasions when masks are not central features of ritual. For instance, in some of the most significant ceremonial complexes dancers did not and do not wear masks. The Cannibal Dancer in the Kwakwaka'wakw Tsetseka, or Winter Ceremonial, wears hemlock branches which, as he calms down, are exchanged for a cedar bark ring. Other, actually lesser, participants in the dance, the Cannibal Bird monsters, wear masks; these are vast, moving

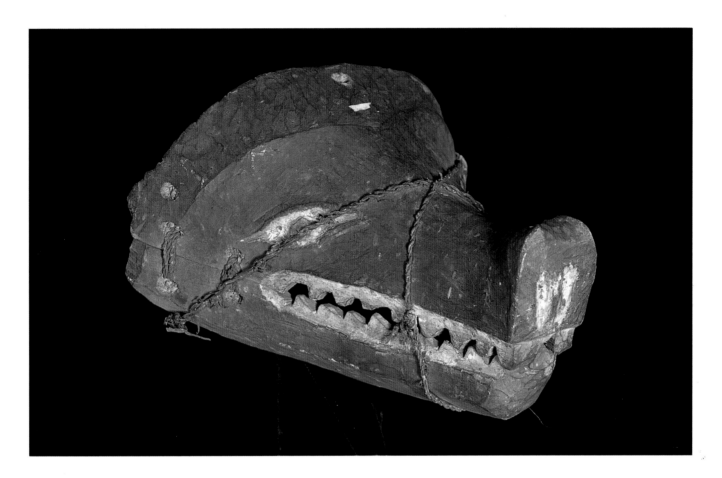

71. Frontlet of wood in the form of a wolf, probably used in one of the dances associated with the Nuu-Chah-Nulth Wolf Ritual. Mid 19th century. L. 21cm.

bird heads painted in sharp colours and carved from red cedar (see fig. 70). Similarly the Wolf Dance of the Southern Wakashans, the Makah and Nuu-Chah-Nulth, involved a performance by a dancer possessed by a wolf – and yet he wore no mask, although lesser participants wore small wolf frontlets (see fig. 71). There is other evidence for the perhaps often marginal significance of masks in Northwest Coast society.

George Hunt, the great part-Tlingit informant of the anthropologist Franz Boas, recorded information to the effect that before the appearance of metal tools only headgear of cedar bark was used by the Kwakwaka'wakw. Intriguingly, neither masks nor mask parts seem to have been recovered from the Makah village of Ozette in the state of Washington, a pre- and proto-historic wet site in which, in a series of mud slides, successive houses were covered and sealed over. Some 50,000 wood artefacts were recovered, mostly in the 1970s. These include decorated and ceremonial materials such as dishes, combs, clubs and the monumental ceremonial carving of a whale saddle. But there are no masks, nor indeed rattles, suggesting that even if these things did exist before European contact they were substantially less common then than was the case later on, although the ceremonials are likely, at least in part, to have already been in existence. Finally, when the Tlingit of Southeast Alaska, commemorated a dead chief, the first four

72. Mask in the form of a wolf, a clan crest of the Tlingit. Collected by Samuel Beeman, a Hudson's Bay Company employee, before 1867. L. 24cm.

'crying feasts' were marked by a complete absence of show; it was only when his successor gave a great potlatch that crest regalia, including masks, would appear.

Masks & potlatches

The central occasion for masking was and is the feast, of which potlatching, or 'giving away' from the Chinook jargon, was the most conspicuous feature. While not all feasts are potlatches all potlatches are feasts, at which claims to crests, names and positions are validated by the observation of guests. The guests are paid for this central contribution to the occasion with goods and, today, with money. In the nineteenth century the potlatch was not in use everywhere on the coast. Instead it spread gradually, growing in a dramatic manner with the foundation of land-based fur trading forts, particularly at Fort Rupert and Port Simpson. These in turn provided opportunities for the accumulation of wealth, and in some societies for competitive feasting at which, in a social order rapidly transformed by trade and disease, social advancement occurred for people not necessarily of high birth.

The primary occasions for potlatching are those of rites of passage: for the birth of the children of chiefs; for the naming of children, or the transfer of names to adults; for marriages; for deaths and, perhaps most often, as memorials to the dead. A potlatch may be given at the moment of the transfer of names from one chief to another, or on the raising of a memorial pole, or the building of a large house. Just as many aspects of ceremonialism spread from the central Northwest Coast southwards, so masking traditions spread too, but they were not significant in all Northwest Coast societies. While the arrival of Europeans brought intensified trade and eventually the cessation of native war, the numerous epidemics resulted in a population collapse from perhaps 200,000 people to less than 20,000 a century later. For some peoples this resulted in the disappearance of potlatching and of masked dances celebrating authority, although individuals and single lineages might continue to hold heirlooms and clan privileges, including masks. In British Columbia masking ceased for the Haida, for instance, more or less completely in the nineteenth century, although it thrives today.

A Canadian law of 1884 forbade potlatching as a wasteful, uncivilised activity, perhaps associated with simulated cannibalism. It was seen as a central impediment to the conversion of Indians into solid Victorian citizens. Bureaucratic uncertainty as to whether the law should be put into effect remained, however, and the Kwakwaka'wakw suffered extensive retribution for continued potlatching during the 1920s. While it remained legal to dance, and to transfer goods from one person to another, it was not permitted to potlatch, that is to dance, feast and give away goods. So

73. (overleaf) Haida helmet representing a creature such as the Sea Grizzly, with a killer whale and ravens attached. L. 45cm.

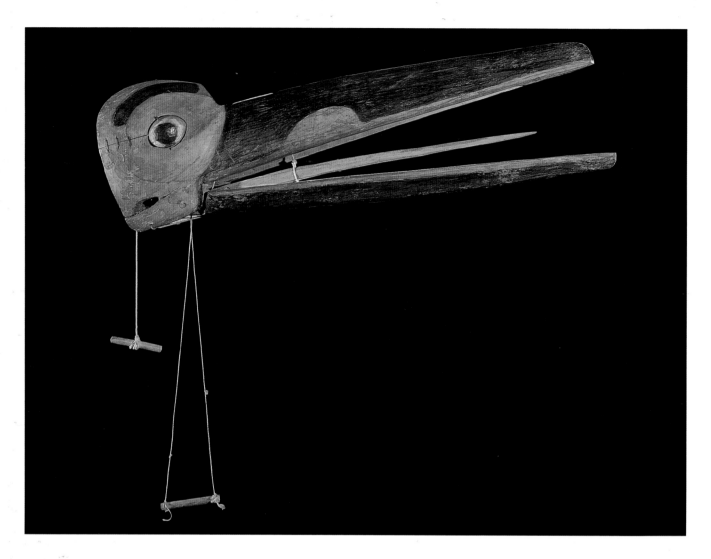

74. Bird mask of wood, Nishga'a, with movable jaw, tongue and eyes. Late nineteenth or early twentieth century, collected on the Nass River, British Columbia. L. 72cm.

75. Mask of wood in the form of a beaver, probably used for a crest among the Tsimshian or other people of the northern coast of British Columbia. H. 23cm.

dancing and gift-giving came to occur separately during the 1930s and 1940s. Much of the demise of potlatching, from the 1930s onwards, came also with economic depression and decline. The lack of access to capital for the purchase of motorised vessels meant that individuals could not play a full role in the commercial fishing industry. Thus they could not obtain the necessary wealth for participation in the ceremonial system. Among other peoples, such as the Nuu-Chah-Nulth, dancing and potlatching continued without a break. For the Kwakwaka'wakw revival came with the building of the Big House at the then British Columbia Provincial Museum in 1953, soon after the effective end of the ban on potlatching in 1951. This was followed by the creation of other new communal Big Houses, particularly that at Alert Bay in 1962. Related to the return of the potlatch was a revival in carving, which was grounded in a partnership between surviving artists, such as Mungo Martin and Bill Reid (who turned back to his Haida heritage), and anthropologists working in museums and universities. Governmental involvement in Northwest Coast art had begun much

76. A transformation mask relating to an unidentified story in which a bear, or other large mammal, turns into a bird of prey, possibly a raven. Northern British Columbia. w. when open: 80 cm.

earlier. In the period from 1876 to 1939 US and Canadian commissions at expositions transported poles, houses and Northwest Coast people for a variety of educational and nationalistic shows. After 1953 carvers, and then family dance groups, entered into commissions for the celebration of governmental objectives, particularly in Canada. Examples of these projects include the erection of a pole carved by Mungo Martin in Windsor Great Park for the 1958 celebration of the centenary of British Columbia, a pole by the artist Norman Tait erected in Bushy Park, London, to celebrate the 125th anniversary of the Canadian Confederation in 1992, and the recent siting of a life-size bronze 'Spirit Canoe' by Bill Reid at the Canadian Embassy in Washington. In all of these projects the use of masks plays a small but vital role, both in the ceremonies associated with the dedication of these things, and in the art which so emphasises the formalised rendition of the face.

Styles and meanings

The central feature of the ceremonial art of the Northwest Coast is the concept of the 'crest' – family, clan or lineage-owned badges – representing

natural phenomena, mythical creatures and ancestors. Many of these are likely to have originated as spirit helpers of individuals, handed down from one generation to another, so that symbols of religious origin may have in time become transformed into symbols of family or political significance. The depiction of crests is usually regarded as deriving from a single art tradition, which developed slowly over thousands of years throughout the whole coast area among people of disparate linguistic origin who shared common hunting and subsistence traditions. Separate sculptural traditions arose among each of the Northwest Coast peoples. At the centre of these are formalised treatments of the human face. These carving styles were employed not merely in the creation of masks but in the adornment of a wide range of paraphernalia from totem poles and canoe prows, to combs, paint brushes and amulets. In many artefacts the sculptural treatment of the face is combined with a two-dimensional, diminutive treatment of the torso and limbs – such as wings, pectoral fins, arms and legs. But in a sense all Northwest Coast art derives from the representation of the face or mask.

Most Northwest Coast sculpture exhibits a dynamic tension between the

77. Mask from the central coast of British Columbia, probably representing a creature or spirit in the Winter Ceremonial. H. 29cm.

78. Wood mask with movable mouth and eyes said to have been collected near Sitka, from Tlingit territory. However, it is most likely to have been associated originally with the Kwakwaka'wakw Winter Ceremonial further to the south. H. 24cm.

form represented and the raw material, whether it be a tree trunk or a bear tooth. Often the artist seeks both to maximise the potential of the raw material and to pass beyond its limitations. This is best exemplified by Kwakwaka'wakw artists, who would utilise the form of a wood block to the full and then add separate wings, beaks or whatever, to transcend the confines of the wood. Haida and Kwakwaka'wakw carving is characterised by deep bold planes, but whereas Haida sculpture is smooth, curved and almost voluptuous in a calm and considered style, Kwakwaka'wakw carving is expressionist with abrupt jutting planes defining facial features. The carving styles of the Tlingit, Heiltsuk, Haisla, Oweekeno, and Tsimshian-speaking peoples is smoother in a sense and more realistic than that of the Kwakwaka'wakw, the differences being defined by variant facial planes, and by the more restrained treatment of eyes, cheeks and other features. Nuxalk sculpture shares with Kwakwaka'wakw deep expansive planes and hard edges, while Coast Salish mask carving is abstract in a manner not found elsewhere on the coast. Nuu-Chah-Nulth carving contains within it numerous separate traditions, some of which are analogous to those of the Kwakwaka'wakw, with elaborate moving additions to masks; another tradition utilises two acute angular planes, while a third tradition is realistic, employing the shallow naturalistic modelling of facial features.

The complex differences in carving styles are accentuated by variations in painted styles. From the north, emanating from the Tsimshian and Heiltsuk, for instance, came the disciplined logical development of abstract split representation of crests. The system was fully and elegantly explained for the first time by Bill Holm, nearly thirty years ago, in *Northwest Coast Indian Art: an analysis of form* (1965). He described the formalised designs in terms of what he defined as 'formlines', curved, swelling lines, with black for the outline, red for the interior, and the occasional use of blue or green for tertiary elements. The complex jointed figures created within this system were built from a few basic shapes, particularly ovoids and 'U' forms. While these abstract creations are not featured in their most idealised forms on masks, even from the northern Northwest Coast, they did interact both with facial painting, and with the representation of abstract crests on masks. To the south, and particularly among the Kwakwaka'wakw, the subtleties of painting in two or three colours were replaced this century with the striking, indeed almost strident, use of black, white and red enamel paints. These may seem harsh colours in the fluorescent light of a museum storeroom, but when danced – suffused with the glow from the central fire of a Big House – they may attain a dramatic, purposeful quality.

Masks in ceremonial

The ceremonials associated with Kwakwaka'wakw masked performances are perhaps the most elaborate of any on the Northwest Coast. They are

79. Mask in the form of Noohlmahl, a grotesque creature covered in matted hair and mucus, important in Kwakwaka'wakw ceremonialism. Collected at Fort Rupert, British Columbia, before 1875. H. 27cm.

neither merely a form of acting, nor entertainment, but instead represent a projection of graded privileges from their holders or owners onto the people participating as invited witnesses. This is as true today as it was in the second half of the nineteenth century. Masks are an important part of these performances but can scarcely be considered separately from not only other material paraphernalia but also owned songs and names and other non-material aspects of rank. Kwakwaka'wakw ceremonial has traditionally mostly taken place in the winter – the Tsetseka ceremonial season. The ceremonial complexes have often been thought of as secret societies, into which individuals are initiated. The central feature of the winter or 'cedar bark dance' was the possession of the initiate by spirits such as those of Bakbakwalanooksiwae, the man-eating spirit, or Winalagilis, the warrior spirit. Formerly when possession by the spirit occurred, the initiate or recipient would disappear from the community for a prolonged period of time. This no longer happens.

Once the masks and food are prepared the invited high-ranking guests assemble. In the initial stages mourning songs are sung, and other dances and hereditarily-owned masked performances might be mounted. The climax of the ceremonial is the return of the possessed dancer from Bakbakwalanooksiwae, the cannibal dancer seeking to eat flesh. The dancer might bite the guests, and perhaps appear to indulge in the eating of human flesh. He would be progressively tamed, eventually being accompanied by his female relations dancing and honouring him. One climax in the sequence was the appearance of Bakbakwalanooksiwae's associates, dancers wearing large cannibal bird masks, one of which is called Hokhokw (see fig. 70). These, like other mythological creatures, have their origins in stories associated with specific individuals and animal species. In one account a chief was bear hunting by himself; after he had been away four days he saw a Hokhokw, which is said to be similar to a crane, although larger than a human. The bird came after the chief and tried to eat him, but the chief escaped home where he took the bird as a crest, proclaiming this right at a potlatch. The Noohlmahl (see fig. 79) is another formidable mythological creature, filthy, with long matted hair and a big nose, whose masked performance requires comment from the guests, although any reference to his filthy nose may produce a violent, unpredictable response. Many other masked dance sequences occurred during the Tsetseka, including that of the Tokwit, a female war spirit who brought out demonstrations of supernatural spirits characterised by elaborate sleights of hand, including the appearance of vast birds, large frogs and a demonstration of immortality after decapitation or death by fire. At the end of all these ceremonials the guests, acting also as participant witnesses, were paid and goods distributed.

Much of the Kwakwaka'wakw winter ceremonial was acquired in the

80. Mask of a cannibal creature from the Kwakwaka'wakw Winter Ceremonial. Collected in the 1860s. L. 28cm.

middle of the nineteenth century when Fort Rupert Kwakwaka'wakw massacred a group of Heiltsuk chiefs from Bella Bella who had come to invite the Kwakwaka'wakw to a potlatch. The Heiltsuk, Haisla and Oweekeno peoples both influenced and were influenced by their neighbouring Tsimshian-speaking peoples, and also by the Haida. For the Haida the two main occasions for potlatching, and therefore, incidentally, for masked performances, were the ceremonials undertaken for the celebration of the completion of a communal house with its frontal pole (the last of which occurred in 1881) and the mortuary potlatch. The former was an occasion not just for the acknowledgement of the assistance given by the people building the house, but also for the proclamation of the status of the children, with the transfer of names and crest tattoos from the house owner to his progeny. Generally in this area masked performances were contributed both by shamans, and by, for instance, those already initiated into Heiltsuk ceremonial societies. Haida acquisition of these rights was, like the Kwakwaka'wakw acquisition of Heiltsuk rituals, perhaps by copying rather than more appropriate transfer. Among the three or four Tsimshian-speaking peoples, the most important potlatches included those for mourning, particularly the last in a sequence of three, in which an heir assumes the position of his predecessor, and those for proclaiming a name, to validate a crest or raise a totem pole.

All over the Northwest Coast a central aspect of mythology is the intermarriage of women and animals. Among northern peoples, such as the Tlingit and Haida, stories tell of marriage with bears. Among the Nuu-Chah-Nulth and Makah of Vancouver Island and Washington, such marriages are said to occur with wolves. The right to tell these stories, and to pass them down with associated privileges, rested, as elsewhere, in specific families. Called the Kluwana (or numerous dialectic variants) among the Nuu-Chah-Nulth, the Wolf Ritual played a similar role as the private ceremonials of the Kwakwaka'wakw. The long feast, which might last eight days or more, served to introduce young people to the rights and obligations inherent in their position. It also emphasised solidarity within the family and group, by for instance incorporating into the proceedings the public ridicule of unacceptable behaviour – such as that of warring couples. The dancing associated with the Wolf Ritual introduced numerous eclectic masking privileges, which, unlike the Wolf Ritual itself, survive today. As elsewhere on the coast a host of animals such as eagle, raven, crane, snipe, bears and felines appear, usually with masks (see fig. 71). These have forms which, although carved in a specific Nuu-Chah-Nulth style, are recognisably the same creatures as elsewhere. Yet in each case the stories associated with the specific masking privileges may be unique and unrelated to those of other peoples. One important form of headgear is the headdress associated with Haetlik, or Lightning Serpent, the belt of

81. (*opposite*) Frontlet for headdress, possibly Nuxalk, carved with a raven surrounded by five bear-like heads. The eyes are formed from bolt heads. H. 27.5cm.

82. Halkomelem *Sxwayxwey* mask of wood in the form of a bird, collected at Nanaimo. Presented to the Christy Collection by Frederick Whymper, the artist on the Vancouver Island Exploring Expedition of 1864. H. 45cm.

the Thunderbird, a mythological creature often represented with the features of an eagle.

In contrast to the Nuu-Chah-Nulth, the Coast Salish peoples of southern British Columbia and northern Washington possess one masked dance complex. This is the *Sxwayxwey*, meaning perhaps 'the flying-around-one' or 'whirlwind dance'. It is associated particularly with the Halkomelem who live towards the southern end of Vancouver Island (see fig. 82). The dance is performed with masks often possessing the features of birds, but which represent creatures probably known only to the separate commissioners of this article of paraphernalia. The Nuxalk are also Salishan-speaking people, traditionally living on the deep inlets on the northern coast of British Columbia (see fig. 81). As elsewhere, their masking tra-

83. Helmet of wood, in the form of a raven, a Tlingit crest. The bird is shown holding the sun, which it obtained for the world by trickery. L. at base: 44cm.

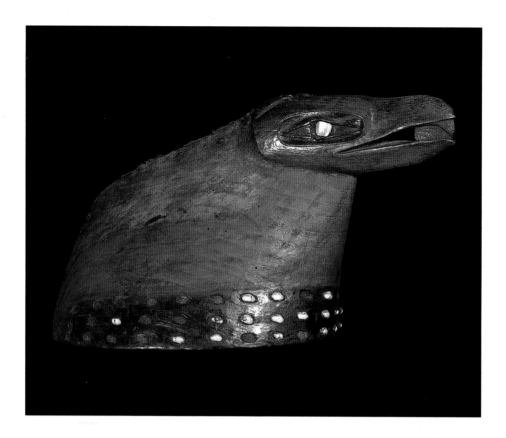

84. (*opposite*) Frontlet for a headdress, Tlingit, carved with the beaver crest and inlaid with abalone shell. H. 19cm

ditions derive from ceremonials both similar and related to those of neighbouring people, particularly the Heiltsuk. Other ceremonials may come from the Kwakwaka'wakw. Of particular importance are the Sisaok and Kusiut Societies, into which people would be inducted in the winter months. In the Kusiut society the novice would be initiated in one season and first perform the following year. Over the several days of the dance songs would be composed and masks created. Both the dances, such as the Cannibal and Scratcher dances, and the mask names such as Thunder and Laughter, derived from borrowed or acquired performances and from natural phenomena.

There were two opportunities for Tlingit masking, as in other Northwest Coast societies. Either masks might be worn at potlatches commemorating rites of passage, or else they were associated with shamans and their spirit helpers. Potlatches were held at three main times: at funerals, at memorials and at the ear-piercing ceremonies of noble children. As elsewhere, elements of different occasions might be combined in a single feast, so that while a potlatch might be held as a memorial for the dead ancestors of a specific chief, it would also celebrate living clan members. An important element of these feasts, which might last several days, would be feasts with dancing in imitation of clan crests, and perhaps dancing with shaman-like masks. The shaman – usually but not always a man – was a dominating personality within the community. His or her role was to control forces of

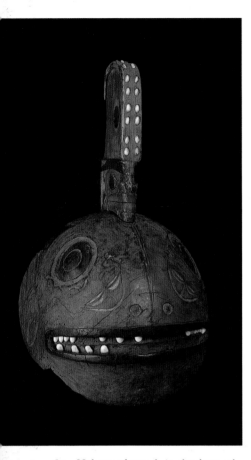

85. Helmet of wood, in the form of a killer whale, a Tlingit crest, decorated with copper, snail shell opercula and human hair. Nineteenth century. L. without hair: 28cm.

86. Frontlet of wood inlaid with California abalone in the form of a hawk, associated with Chief Kadashan of the Tlingit. H. 18.5cm.

both natural and human origin for the benefit of individuals or the whole lineage. In cases of prolonged illness a shaman from another clan and community might be called upon, since the illness might have been caused by a relation who was also a witch. The shaman would then seek to locate the witch, and obtain a confession. A shaman's paraphernalia included masks, amulets and rattles, all of which might be buried with him. His (or her) power came from the spirits believed to inhabit living and non-living things. The mask was the most powerful component of shamanic paraphernalia. Each shaman would possess four masks, one for each spirit, although the most powerful individuals might possess eight masks. These would be basically human in form, but with specific attributes which would identify the personal spirit. The creatures might include shark, octopus and hawk, perhaps with an additional spirit or *yake* incorporated in the carving. Shamanic masks tended to have a less dramatic appearance and smaller form than Tlingit family crests, which were owned by clans.

The forms of Tlingit headgear and masking paraphernalia were extremely varied, and included crest frontlets attached to headdresses (see figs 84, 86), spruce-root hats painted with crests, and, at the time of European contact, crest helmets worn in time of war (see figs 83, 85). Some of these forms were acquired from the Haida and Tsimshian to the south.

The impact of European contact

With the arrival of Europeans in the last quarter of the eighteenth century, Northwest Coast society was subjected to intense pressures. The destructive impact of disease, alcohol and the maritime fur trade was combined with the sudden availability of copious amounts of metal tools and vast arrays of objects of new wealth, including, in particular, manufactured textiles, rifles and other exotic weapons. During the nineteenth century successive phases of European contact – the maritime fur trade, the land-based fur trade, and then commercial fishing and European-American canneries – created wealth, but it was twinned with catastrophic population decline. The resultant rapid changes in Northwest Coast society allowed for developments both in the art style, and in the transfer of dances, with their associated masking traditions, from one people to the next. Nevertheless, new carving styles, created in periods of rapid social and economic transition, were sufficiently stable for coherent traditions to be created and maintained. The principles of nineteenth century Northwest Coast art, as first defined by Franz Boas, were elaborated by Bill Holm, so as to define its elements. This was achieved so that both scholars interested in the art form and carvers and artists working with wood and paint would comprehend the work of the great masters of northern Northwest Coast art.

Today while many masks are made for use, most are created for sale to non-natives, plaques often seen as lifeless representations of crests,

NOTE
In accordance with contemporary usage the following preferred names are used for British Columbia peoples: Kwakwaka'wakw for the Southern Kwakiutl or Kwakiutl; Heiltsuk, Haisla and Oweekeno for the Northern Kwakiutl; Nuxalk for the Bella Coola, and Nuu-Chah-Nulth for the Nootka.

designed never to be worn and used. As a result of the increase in carving, after the nadir of the 1940s and 1950s, skills were acquired by literally hundreds of natives. They turned to this specialised form of creativity, both as a livelihood and as a means of participating in a traditional activity which was both founded in the wider economy, and expressive of continued participation in an ancient heritage. Most artefacts made for sale are masks, and many of the silk screen prints produced by the one or two British Columbia printers depict masks. Northwest Coast humanoid masks, with totem poles, provide icons of cultural survival taken by the tourist tides and swept around the world.

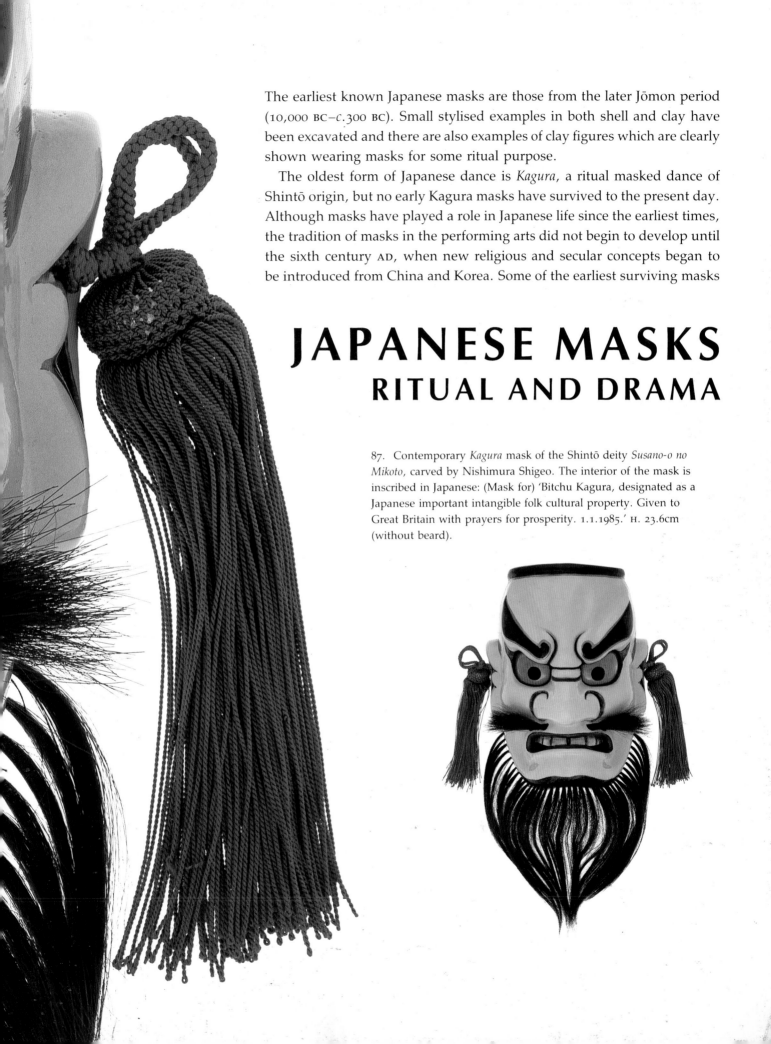

The earliest known Japanese masks are those from the later Jōmon period (10,000 BC–c.300 BC). Small stylised examples in both shell and clay have been excavated and there are also examples of clay figures which are clearly shown wearing masks for some ritual purpose.

The oldest form of Japanese dance is *Kagura*, a ritual masked dance of Shintō origin, but no early Kagura masks have survived to the present day. Although masks have played a role in Japanese life since the earliest times, the tradition of masks in the performing arts did not begin to develop until the sixth century AD, when new religious and secular concepts began to be introduced from China and Korea. Some of the earliest surviving masks

JAPANESE MASKS
RITUAL AND DRAMA

87. Contemporary *Kagura* mask of the Shintō deity *Susano-o no Mikoto*, carved by Nishimura Shigeo. The interior of the mask is inscribed in Japanese: (Mask for) 'Bitchu Kagura, designated as a Japanese important intangible folk cultural property. Given to Great Britain with prayers for prosperity. 1.1.1985.' H. 23.6cm (without beard).

88. Gigaku mask, probably of *Shishiko*, one of the two young attendants of the mythical *Shishi*. The mask is carved from a single piece of camphor wood with some pigment remaining on a gesso base, giving a flesh colour; real hair is fixed with adhesive to the crown of the head. H. 29.3cm.

are those used for the dance drama known as *Gigaku*. Around the same time as the arrival of Gigaku, another form of dance was gradually being introduced from mainland Asia. This was *Bugaku*, which is still performed in Japan today. Alongside their use in dance and drama, masks began to appear in Buddhist temple processions during the eighth and ninth centuries. During the fourteenth century the uniquely Japanese *Nō* mask became fully developed along with the more comical *Kyōgen* mask.

Masks today are still found at festivals, depicting traditional Japanese characters and children's comic book heroes. In addition, the art of carving continues with contemporary artists producing fine works, notably in the field of Nō and Kagura masks.

Kagura

Kagura is a type of performance or ritual shamanistic dance which has Shintō origins. Shintō is a religion (or set of folk beliefs) with its roots in the relationship between the land and the people dependent upon it. Most forms of Kagura are connected with fertility rites, and offer performances to the gods to ensure a plentiful harvest. The tradition of Kagura is still flourishing in modern-day Japan, with masked performances found throughout the country, usually at Shintō shrines, on important occasions such as harvest time or at New Year festivals. The masks feature the popular deities of Shintoism.

The legendary origin of Kagura is described in the *Kojiki* (Record of Ancient Matters, AD 712) which tells of an amusingly erotic dance performed by the goddess Ame no Uzume to entice the Sun goddess, Amaterasu Ōmikami, out of hiding. The offensive behaviour of Susano-o no Mikoto, the younger brother of Amaterasu, had driven the Sun goddess into a cave, bringing darkness and disaster upon the world. Susano-o was banished from the High Celestial Plain and descended to what is now Izumo, in western Japan. Here he found that a monster, the Yamata no Orichi, had killed and eaten seven of the daughters of an elderly couple and was demanding their eighth. He gave the monster rice wine and, while it was drunkenly sleeping, slew it. The British Museum has a contemporary mask of Susano-o no Mikoto (fig. 87) and the companion mask of the eighth daughter in this tale, both carved by the same maker.

Gigaku

By tradition, Gigaku was brought to Japan around AD 550 by Chisō, a member of the royal family of Wu, a kingdom in central China. He brought with him Buddhist writings and artefacts, and Gigaku masks, costumes and instruments, but apparently not the dance itself. It was not until AD 612 that we have the first record of an actual performance of Gigaku. This was when Mimashi, a Korean who had learned Gigaku in Wu, came to

Japan with a number of Gigaku masks which still survive today at the Hōryū temple in Nara. Prince Shōtoku Taishi invited Mimashi to come to Nara to teach Gigaku and, under his patronage, Gigaku came to play an important role at the Imperial court and also in large Buddhist temples. Some masks preserved at the Shōsō-in (the Imperial repository) are inscribed with the date of the consecration of the Great Buddha sculpture at the Tōdai temple in Nara in AD 752.

From a later record, the *Kyōkunshō*, written in AD 1233, we have some idea of the form of a Gigaku performance. Masks were carried in procession with musical accompaniment around a temple courtyard. The procession was led by Chidō, a character with a long-nosed mask, performing a ritual cleansing of the route. He was followed by a *shishi*, a mythical creature consisting of a lion mask attached to a length of cloth and operated by two men, and escorted by two young masked attendants called *shishiko*. They performed a ritual dance and offered prayers. The play which followed featured the king of Wu, Gokō, and his beautiful daughter Gojo, who became the focus of attention for Konron, an evil-looking character. Konron danced while beating a phallic stick called a *marakata* and then caught hold of Gojo. Kongō, a Buddhist guardian, and Rikishi, a wrestler, grappled and defeated Konron. The performance was a precept against lust: Konron, the embodiment of lust and therefore an obstacle to enlightenment, is overcome by the guardians of Buddhism.

Other plays are documented, all of them in some way moralistic: *Baramon* (Brahman) a high-caste monk who fathers a child and must redeem himself and repent, dances with long pieces of cloth to represent washing the child's soiled clothes; *Taiko*, in which Taikofu and the child Taikoji offer prayers before Buddha as a rite for the dead; and *Suiko*, in which a foreign king and his attendants dance in a boisterous, drunken fashion (most likely as a warning against intoxication). All the characters in Gigaku are masked, and the performances are accompanied by the lively music of flutes, drums and cymbals.

Gigaku masks have facial characteristics which are not of Japanese origin, but show influences from mainland Asia, in particular India and China. The mask of Suiko, however, has strong Persian features. The masks fit over the face and head of the wearer and are carved in the round, being almost sculptural in appearance. A mask of the Nara period (AD 645–781) in the British Museum (fig. 88) is most probably that of a shishiko, as it is child-sized (28.9 cm) and can be compared with similar contemporary examples in the Tōdai temple.

The decline of Gigaku in the Heian period (AD 782-1184) and its replacement by the more austere Bugaku drama and Gyōdō processions was due mostly to the reduction in ties with mainland Asia, as Japan adapted the Buddhist influences which had been absorbed so readily during the earlier

Nara period. Several characters from Gigaku have influenced later masked performances, and the *shishimai* or lion dance is still to be found in Buddhist processions and in popular festivals today.

Bugaku

Bugaku is the dance form of the orchestral tradition known as Gagaku, and both derive from forms in use in the T'ang court in China (seventh–tenth centuries AD). The forms of dance adopted by the Japanese Imperial court were divided into styles which indicated from which region they had been collected by the T'ang court, for example Korea (*Kōraigaku*), Manchuria (*Bokkaigaku*), or India (*Tenjikugaku*). The different forms created a rich and complex drama.

In the Heian period, Bugaku was systematically organised into the form in which it can be seen today. In the eleventh century the forms of Bugaku were separated into dances of the Left (*Samai*, using T'ang music and dance) and dances of the Right (*Umai*, using Korean, Manchurian and Japanese music and dance). The Left and Right had their own clearly-defined dance movements, costume colours and musical instruments. The music for the dances of the Left was generally more cheerful than that of the Right. At this time Bugaku would have been performed at court during feasts, for Imperial audiences and at temples for purification ceremonies. In comparison with Gigaku, the orchestra for a Bugaku performance was large, consisting of three types of drums, flute, *shō* (a type of circular droning mouth organ), *koto* (a type of horizontal harp), *biwa* (lute), *shōko* (gong) and *hichiriki* (flageolet).

Bugaku was always regarded as the dance of the Imperial court. In the *Tale of Genji* there are detailed descriptions of how the music and dance of the court formed an integral part of Heian aristocratic life. There are documented tales of a young prince moving an audience to tears with his performance of Ryō-ō, as well as that of a performance of Nasori by the nine-year-old son of a court minister. Bugaku was performed both by nobles who valued it as part of their education and by those in the hereditary guilds of professional musicians. Many of the members of today's Imperial Palace Music Department are directly descended from those of the original eighth-century guilds.

In the Kamakura period (AD 1185–1332), the power of the nobles faded and Gagaku and Bugaku declined as art forms. The centres of Bugaku were dispersed to the temples and shrines of Nara and Kyōto and to the Shittenō temple in Ōsaka. Bugaku was later revitalised in the Edo period (AD 1600–1867) under the Tokugawa Shōgunate. After the Meiji restoration (AD 1868) and the formation of the Music Department of the Imperial Household Agency, the traditions were once again united under Imperial patronage. Public performances of Bugaku can be seen today in Nara, at Nikkō

90. Ryō-ō, the Dragon King, from a handscroll dated to 1816, showing Bugaku dances at the Tōshōgū Shrine in Nikkō. The traditional robes for the role are clearly shown in the painting, and despite their bulk, the actor gives a vigorous performance.

89. Bugaku mask of Ryō-ō, the Dragon King. Made of cypress wood, it has been finely carved, lacquered and gilded with real hair added to the beard and moustache. The chin is suspended by silk cords, the eyes are held in place by a metal rod to which the cords are attached. H.33.5cm (excluding chin plate).

Tōshōgū (the shrine to the first Tokugawa Shōgun), at the Shitteno temple in Ōsaka, and at the Imperial Palace in Tōkyō.

The masks of Bugaku differ from Gigaku in that they are generally more dramatic and stylised, and as the performances were livelier, the masks were constructed to allow greater freedom of movement. They are smaller and lighter and cover only the face and sides of the head. A unique feature of many masks is that they have movable parts such as noses, eyes or chins, occasionally used in combination. This serves to heighten the dramatic, or sometimes comic, aspects of a performance. In the play *Kotokuraku* (which in many ways resembles the Gigaku play *Suiko*), the masks have movable noses, which as the play progresses are used to great effect to show the increasing drunkenness of the characters. There are many Heian period masks preserved in temples and museums in Japan, often repaired or repainted but still retaining their original character.

The British Museum has an Edo period Bugaku mask of Ryō-ō (fig. 89), which still has its original lacquered and brocaded box. The dragon is carved so that it crouches low on top of the mask to form a kind of helmet. The chin and eyes move in harmony to emphasise the rhythm of the dance.

The story of Ryō-ō, the Dragon King, is based on the tale of Ranryō, a handsome young Chinese prince of the sixth century who went into battle wearing a ferocious mask in order to terrify his enemies and avoid distracting his allies with his beauty. One story relating to the performance of Ryō-ō tells of a unique somersaulting technique used by the actor, a difficult task while wearing the costume and mask for this part. The illustration of Ryō-ō in a handscroll dated to 1816 (fig. 90) gives some idea of the vitality of this performance.

Masks in Buddhist ceremonies

The use of masks in Buddhist ceremonies began in the Nara period with the introduction of practices from the T'ang court, in which a holy image, normally kept unseen in a temple, is paraded through the streets. The image was accompanied by attendants wearing masks depicting Buddhist deities, often that of Bosatsu, a Bodhisattva, who postpones the ultimate state of enlightenment in order to help with the salvation of mankind (fig. 92). It is known that Bosatsu masks were worn as part of a Bugaku ceremony at the consecration of the Great Buddha at the Tōdai temple, in AD 752. Gradually the Bosatsu dance was absorbed into a purely Buddhist ceremony known as Gyōdō, or Kamen-Gyōdō.

The earliest form of Gyōdō ceremony consisted of a procession of monks who circled the temple while chanting sutras. It is possible that this practice originated in India, where certain Buddhist rituals took the form of circumambulation. The *Shōryō* ceremony, which is believed to date from the Nara period and is still performed at the Hōryū temple, consists of a procession

91. Participants in the Buddhist procession known as Nerikuyo. The person wearing the Gyōdō mask is part of a group representing various Bodhisattvas, and is assisted as he walks the temple precincts accompanying the image of Amida Buddha. This particular event was recorded at Taimadera in Nara, where it is sometimes performed as a memorial service for a devout Buddhist.

bearing the ashes of Prince Shōtoku (Shōtoku Taishi, AD 572–622, patron saint of Japanese Buddhists) and his statue. The palanquin bearing these relics is carried by eight men wearing masks representing the attendants of the Buddha.

Gyōdō masks are also worn at a ceremony known as *Raigō*, a re-enactment of the descent of Amida. This ceremony is associated with the *Jōdo*, or Pure Land sect of Buddhism. Jōdo began in the tenth century when the priest Enshin preached that Buddha would descend from paradise to greet the dying who have had faith in Amida Buddha, and lead them to the Western Paradise of Pure Land Buddhism. In this ceremony a procession wearing masks of Bodhisattvas proceeds along a raised bridge from the Amida hall (the centre of the temple complex) to a subsidiary building, returning slowly to the Amida hall. A ceremony known as *Nerikuyo* is a

92. Late Muromachi period Gyōdō mask of Bosatsu, a Bodhisattva who having attained enlightenment remains on earth to help mankind. The mask is constructed from several pieces of wood and fits around most of the wearer's head. It is in the Kamakura style of Buddhist sculpture and conveys a calm, serene and spiritual feeling. The mask is painted white over a black lacquer base, and is gilded in parts. There are traces of red pigment around the mouth and green pigment on the hair and ears. An opaque crystal urna is fixed on the forehead. H. 23.3cm.

part of the Raigō ceremony, and is held today in many temples such as Taimadera in Nara (fig. 91).

The masks in Gyōdō are usually reproductions of Buddhist sculptures and as such are restrained and calm in appearance. The overall impression of the ceremony is that the sculptures in the temple have come to life, giving the devotee a glimpse of the world to come.

The lion dance

The *shishimai*, or lion dance, appears in many forms today. Its origins lie in mainland Asia, and most Asian countries still have some form of lion dance, probably the best-known being in New Year festival processions. Japanese *shishi* masks were originally used in Gigaku, Gyōdō and even in Bugaku.

93. Nineteenth-century festival mask of a *shishi*, a mythical form of lion. It is decorated in red and black lacquer and gilded on the eyes, eyebrows and teeth. It has multicoloured hair as well as a movable tongue and jaw. The mask was worn by one person who worked the jaw, while two others hid under a cloth forming the lion's body. Together they performed a lively dance. Some of the earliest shishi masks dating from the twelfth century are rather dignified in appearance, while later examples, such as this from the Edo period, are somewhat gaudier and often rather comical. H. 34cm.

Early shishi masks such as those in the Shōsō-in date back to the twelfth century. They convey something of the dignity and power of the lion from which the mythical shishi derives. Later masks tended to be rather gaudy and to emphasise the fearsome nature of the lion, this being more suited to the popular use of the shishimai as a form of exorcism. When appearing in popular festivals they even tended towards the comical (fig. 93).

Nō and Kyōgen

Perhaps the most well-known Japanese masks are those for the uniquely Japanese theatre of Nō. Nō, the tragic form of the drama, and Kyōgen, its more comic side, grew out of the earlier folk performances of *Dengaku* and *Sarugaku*, both of which used masks. The flowering of Nō as a dramatic art form came in the fourteenth and fifteenth centuries under the two great actors Kan'ami (1333–84) and his son Zeami (1363–1443).

Dengaku was originally a religious performance derived from rice-planting and harvesting rituals, Sarugaku a lively art form brought over from China which included juggling and acrobatics in its repertoire. The masks for these performances had their origins in Gigaku, the music came from Kagura and the Buddhist liturgy, and the dance from Bugaku. Dengaku was popular with the military class of the Kamakura period but was gradually replaced by Sarugaku which by the late thirteenth century had started to standardise the words, music and gestures of the performances. It was from this art form that Kan'ami and Zeami created the Nō drama as it is performed today.

In 1374 Kan'ami and Zeami performed at the Imagumano shrine in Kyōto before Shōgun Ashikaga Yoshimitsu (1358–1408). Yoshimitsu was a believer in Zen Buddhism and under his patronage Zeami created the foundations of an austere Nō drama based on the Zen principles of restraint, understatement, economy of movement and frugality of expression. Zeami fashioned a number of plays, and wrote a series of treatises on his principles of Nō which have become the foundation of all subsequent performances of this theatre.

The civil wars which started in 1467 brought disruption to performances around Kyōto, but had the effect of dispersing the art of Nō. Around 1500, amateur performances became popular and instruction was provided by the Kanze school, which had descended from Zeami's original troupe of actors. The revival of Nō came about with the support of the Regent Toyotomi Hideyoshi (1537–98), who came to power in 1582 and succeeded in pacifying Japan in 1590. He put all four surviving troupes of actors on his payroll, had them perform for his troops and also commissioned and acted in plays himself. By this time Nō had become far removed from the austerity of Zeami's ideals, to the extent that even the Jesuit missionaries resident in Japan at that time performed Christian Nō.

When Tokugawa Ieyasu came to power in 1603, establishing the Tokugawa Shōgunate, he celebrated with Nō performances and took all of Hideyoshi's actors to his new capital of Edo, modern day Tōkyō. Nō became a ceremonial art form for the Tokugawa family. In 1647 Tokugawa Iemitsu ordered that all the traditions of Nō had to be maintained without variation. The plays were written down, stage directions were firmly established, the costumes and masks were all clearly defined. For the rest of the Edo period (1600–1867) Nō became more austere and solemn, and the performances even slower. Because it was the official music and drama of the Shōgunate, it was rarely seen by the common people. With the fall of the Shōgun in 1867 and the withdrawal of government support, Nō went into decline but was kept alive by Umewaka Minoru (1828–1909). After the Second World War, Nō was revitalised and for the first time became widely available to the public.

Although most stages are today housed in modern buildings, they retain the appearance of the original open-air structures. The layout and use of the stage was formalised in the Edo period with the musicians and actors having fixed positions. There are few stage props; many are mere sugges-

94. Contemporary Nō mask of Okina by Ujiharu Nagasawa. The mask with its hinged lower jaw is reminiscent of the earlier Bugaku masks. The tradition of carving Nō masks is still important in Japan. The work of this particular carver was selected in 1979 as a designated conservation technique necessary for the preservation of Important Intangible Cultural Properties, of which Nō is one of the recognised categories. H. 18.5cm.

tions of objects or are in miniature. Time and space are transmutable: an actor can move a few metres to suggest a long journey, or a brief moment can become a month.

The major character in a play is called the *shite*, and it is only the *shite* and his companions who wear masks, unless they are portraying living characters. All roles whether male, female, deity or demon are acted by men, although a boy actor (*kokata*) is sometimes used for roles such as an Emperor (where the appearance of an adult actor in the role of such a high-ranking person would detract from the central role portrayed by the *shite*). The masks are used in a variety of plays to express the concept of *yūgen*, a quality difficult to define but including grace, darkness and mystery. In the words of the Buddhist priest and poet Shōtetsu, 'what we call yūgen lies within the mind . . . it may be suggested by the veil of a cloud over the moon or by the mists of autumn on the mountainside.'

The oldest performance in the Nō repertoire is that of Okina (fig. 94), which featured in performances as early as the tenth century. The play consists of dances offering prayers for peace, fertility and longevity and is probably Shintō in origin. It is sometimes called the first play, and is performed only on special occasions. It is unique in that it is the only Nō play in which the actor puts on the mask *after* he has appeared on stage. The performance is in several parts, the last being a Kyōgen dance called Sambasō in which the performer wears a mask almost identical to that of Okina except that it is black.

With the exception of Okina, the plays in Nō can be broadly divided into five categories. The first of these is *Kami Nō*, in which the major role is usually a deity (*Kami*). In the first scene the deity appears in human form, often telling of the origin of a shrine or temple. In the second scene he reappears in his true form and performs an auspicious dance. The second category of plays is known as *Shura Nō*, or battle plays, and deals with ghosts from the Genji-Heike wars of the twelfth century, a period in Japanese history which featured many heroic figures and which gave rise to a form of romantic literature. The third category is known as *Kazura Nō*, or 'wig' plays which deal mostly with beautiful women of the Heian period who are obsessed by love. This group was regarded by Zeami as the most important. It features many exquisite dances, and presents the actor with some of his most challenging roles. The fourth group, *Zatsu*, or miscellaneous Nō, includes tragedies of living people and plays dealing with lunacy or obsessions. The plays dealing with living people are very dramatic in style. The lunatic plays typically concern the madness of a woman who has lost her child or lover, and the obsession plays deal with ghosts and spirits unable to leave this world due to strong attachments. This group tends to have more movement on stage than plays from the other groups. The last category of plays is called *Kiri* (final) *Nō* or *Kichiku* (demon) *Nō*

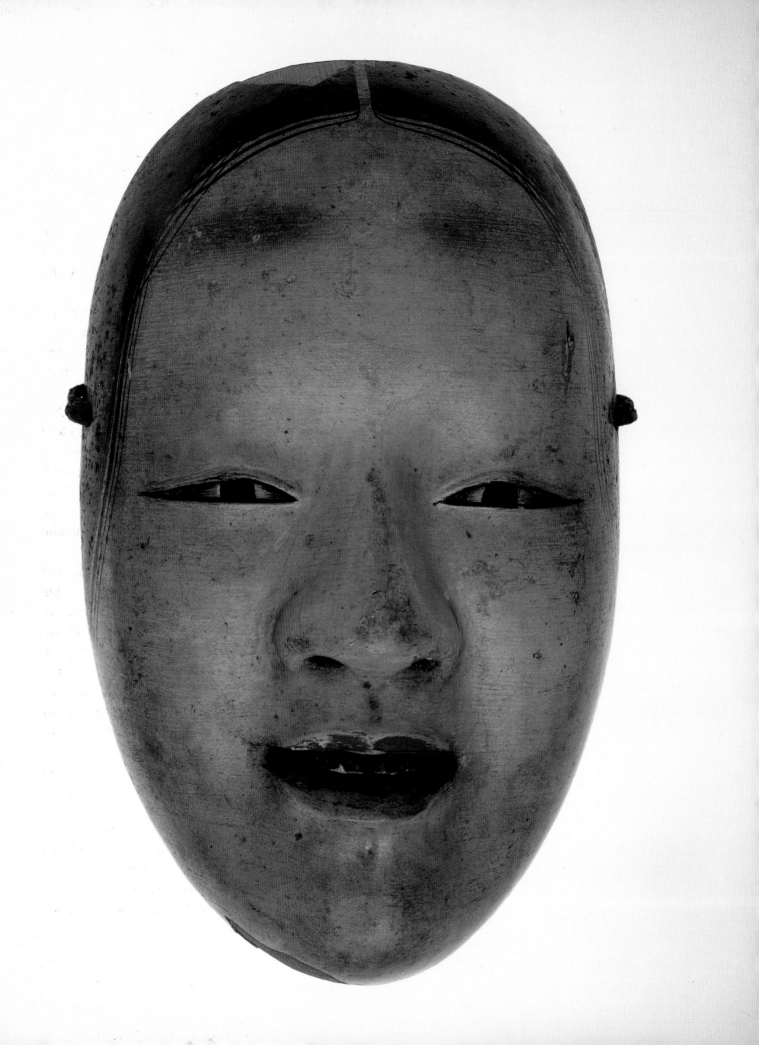

95. Nō mask of Waka Onna, the interior branded with the seal of Deme Taiman. Portraying the characters of young women presents the male actor with some of the most challenging roles in the repertoire of Nō. He must totally convince the audience of the part he is playing. The conventions of Nō mean that the voice is not modified to take into account the age or sex of the character. The mask must convey most of the emotions and it is the skill of the performer which imbues this inanimate object with life. H. 20.8cm.

96 (page 146) The mask of *Hannya* is one of the most well-known masks from Nō. It is used for the character of a jealous and revengeful demon who was once a beautiful woman. The eyes, originally of gilded metal, glare out, the mouth is drawn wide open in a ferocious snarl and the horns embody evil. Only the faint trace of eyebrows high on the forehead and the suggestion of delicate features indicate her former beauty. H. 20.3cm (without horns).

97. (page 147) A *Kishin* (Demon God) dating from the late fifteenth or sixteenth centuries, carved from a single piece of camphor wood. The mask still bears much of the influence of its Gigaku prototype, the barbarian Konron, and has a vitality which is lost in later derivatives of this character. The mask is deeply and vigorously carved with traces of red and black pigment over the remains of the original gesso. Infra-red photography of the mask's interior shows the remains of an unfortunately unreadable signature. H. 23.2cm.

and deals with demons and supernatural beings. They feature fast-moving and dramatic dances concerning the struggle between good and evil.

One of the most dramatic plays in Nō is *Dōjōji* (Dōjō temple). The story tells of the father of a young girl, Kiyohime, who jested that he would marry her off to Anchin, a priest who often visited the family. Kiyohime, when she grew up, tried to persuade the priest to marry her. The priest was forced to flee to his temple and hide under the bronze bell. Kiyohime followed Anchin to the temple where in her anger she was transformed into a raging serpent, which wrapped itself around the bell, killing the priest and melting the bell with the heat of its fury.

The play begins with the inauguration of a new bell at the Dōjō temple. A beautiful girl arrives and, despite the ban on women at the ceremony, charms her way into the temple. She performs a spellbinding dance, at the end of which she slips under the bell which begins to get hot. The priests inform the abbot of what has happened, and he tells them the story of Anchin and Kiyohime. In the first act the *shite* wears the mask of Ōmi Onna, a mask similar to that of Waka Onna (fig. 95), but of a slightly older woman. In the second act the *shite* emerges from beneath the bell wearing the mask of Hannya (fig. 96). The costume too has changed: it is now a design of snake scales. The actor performs a ghostly and dramatic dance. As the dance becomes increasingly furious, the priests pray ever more ardently until, finally, their prayers overcome the evil of Hannya and she disappears.

The masks of Nō are generally neutral in expression, and it is the skill of the actor which brings the mask to life through subtle changes in his physical attitude. The art of the mask carver lies in creating an inanimate object which can be imbued with life. The masks themselves are small and only cover the front of the face, with small eyeholes. After donning his sumptuous costume the actor seats himself before a mirror and studies the mask, becoming one with the character he is about to perform. The mask is then tied onto his head, any wig or necessary headgear is put on and he stands before a full-length mirror letting the mask take over his own personality before he is led to the stage.

Nō masks are invariably carved from a single piece of Japanese cypress wood. The carving alternates from front to back until the desired thickness is reached, then holes are cut for the eyes, nose and mouth. The mask is coated with layers of gesso mixed with glue; it is the sanding down of these layers that gives the mask its final shape. The mask is then painted in the prescribed colours for that particular character. Parts of the mask may be gilded, areas may be highlighted to increase the three-dimensional effect, and some masks have inlaid metallic eyes. The hair and the outline of the eyes are usually finished in black ink.

The British Museum has some thirty Nō masks in the collection, mostly dating from the eighteenth and nineteenth centuries. Notable among its earlier masks is that of a *Kishin*, a fierce god or demon (fig. 97) dating from the later part of the Muromachi period (1392–1572). It is interesting to compare this mask with that of the *Shikami* (fig. 1 in introduction), a later form of this type of demon. The Shikami mask dates from the eighteenth century and although well executed, lacks some of the vigour of the earlier prototype.

Kyōgen is the more humorous side of Nō (which it sometimes parodies)

98. A plastic mask of *Hyottoko*, a character featuring in traditional Kagura performances, but similar to the *Kyōgen Usofuki*. The mask is extremely comical and represents either a man whistling or trying to kindle a fire by blowing on it. The character of Hyottoko is often closely associated with that of Okame, a plump-looking young girl who symbolises prosperity and well-being. The two characters can often be found dancing together at village festivals in Japan. These masks can be bought at the many small stalls which are traditionally found in the precincts of temples and shrines. H. 21.5cm.

and most performances of Nō will have Kyōgen interludes. Kyōgen is performed on the same stage as Nō, and the contrast between the tragic and the comic serves to highlight both techniques of drama. Kyōgen, like Nō, derives from the earlier forms of Dengaku and Sarugaku, but has not been so refined or standardised. Only about fifty Kyōgen plays feature the use of masks. These masks can be broadly divided into those used for the popular gods of Shintō and Buddhism, those for animals, plants or their spirits, and those of human beings, usually rustic characters. Whereas the masks of Nō have a somewhat neutral expression which is brought to life by the actor, those of Kyōgen express their emotions quite openly, and the same mask can be used for a wide variety of characters. The Usofuki mask, for example, which is very similar to the Hyottoko mask of popular festivals (fig. 98), can be used to represent the spirit of a mosquito or a mushroom, as well as a scarecrow, an octopus or a locust.

Other occasions for masking

Apart from its appearance today in traditional Japanese dance and drama, the mask is used for enjoyment at festivals. At these times the reserved (public) persona can be put to one side, as donning the mask of a humorous character releases those inhibitions which normally restrain public

99. Anpanman, a children's comic book character created in 1973 and still popular today. Anpanman is made from a bean-paste bun and constantly battles with his arch enemy Baikinman who tries to spread germs, steal food or pollute the environment. Anpanman helps those who are hungry by giving them part of his bean-paste bun body to eat. The character has spawned a whole industry of Anpanman products, from lunchboxes to full costumes including, of course, the mask.
H. 18.4cm.

behaviour. Children have few such inhibitions and will become totally absorbed in the character they have chosen to adopt. As well as asking for and obtaining the mask of, for example, Anpanman – a recent mild-mannered and educational Japanese children's cartoon character (fig. 99) – the child will try to persuade his parents that the character is incomplete without the rest of the costume. While this reflects a marketing success on the part of the character's creators, the child's attitude is not dissimilar to that of the Nō actor in the dressing room as he prepares to adopt the whole character he is about to portray on stage. A single-mindedness of purpose is evident in both as they prepare to enter, however briefly, a world apart from the mundane reality of life.

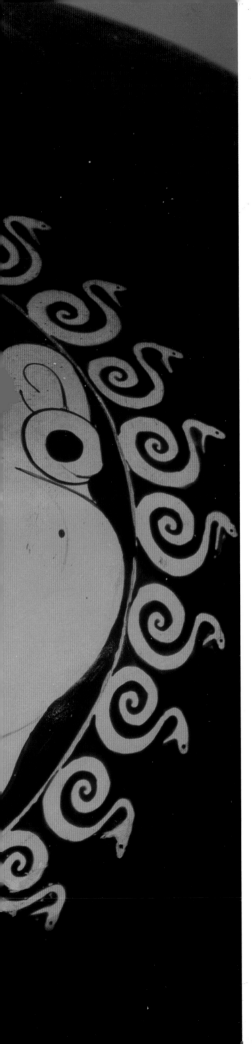

FACE VALUE
THE MASK
IN GREECE
AND ROME

To the ancient Greeks masks were not ambivalent, as we perceive them; rather they were to be taken, as it were, at face value. The Greek word for the face was *to prosopon*, literally 'that which is set before the eye', and the same word was used for a mask. The theatre audience did not sit thrilled in expectation of the mask being lifted to reveal a hidden identity; rather, the mask was a vehicle by which the actor, who was invariably male, even when playing a female part, impersonated his character. In Latin the word for mask is *persona*, and its function was to define the category of the person portrayed. In both the Greek and the Roman theatre the spectator saw only the mask, and the actor's own personality was effaced by it.

This ancient idea of a mask may be contrasted with modern notions as, for example, that of post-Freudian psychology, where it is a metaphor of

100. Scene from a red-figured *hydria* (water jar) made in Athens around 490 BC. The Gorgon Medusa was a mythical monster whose penetrating gaze turned the onlooker to stone. She and her sisters inhabited a land in the far west, at the edge of the world. There Perseus decapitated Medusa, avoiding her stare by employing his polished breastplate as a mirror. According to one version of the story, Perseus was sent to find the Gorgon by the goddess Athena, who afterwards wore the head at the centre of her breastplate or *aegis*. The aegis of Athena, like the head of the Gorgon, was fringed with snakes. With her goggle eyes, bulbous nose, manic grin, vampire fangs and protruding tongue the Gorgon's face is the Greek epitome of nightmare terror. H. of vase 41.6cm.

101. Gustav Klimt, 'Pallas Athena'. The goddess Athena is portrayed by the Viennese painter, Gustav Klimt, as a menacing *femme fatale*. A Corinthian helmet masks her face, and a pair of strange, hypnotic eyes stare out at the viewer. At a time when another prominent Viennese, Sigmund Freud, was attempting to unmask the human mind, Klimt's symbolism suggests a sinister presence behind the goddess's exterior persona.

102. (*opposite*) Scene from a black-figured neck-amphora made in Athens around 530 BC. A warrior falling beneath a chariot turns his head to look out of the picture. At such moments of high drama, Greek vase painters occasionally departed from the convention of showing the human head in profile and portrayed it face-on. The stare of the suffering victim draws our gaze through the helmet masking the face, to concentrate our attention upon the pathos of the moment. H. 43.3cm.

the external self, concealing the reality within. Freud's contemporary, the symbolist painter Gustav Klimt, portrayed the Greek goddess Athena as a *femme fatale* (see fig. 101), whose mysterious countenance with its strangely hypnotic eyes is partly obscured by the nose- and cheek-pieces of a helmet, exploited by the painter as a mask. The mask-like character of the Corinthian helmet was not lost upon the ancient Greeks themselves, but such a use as that in Klimt's painting, where our vision is directed through a mask, is rare in Greek art. When it does occur, its dramatic effect lies in a reversal of the norms governing the function of masks in general.

The helmet covers the face while the wearer is, so to speak, in the battle state. A helmet is to the warrior what the mask is to the actor: the helmet effaces personality to present a stereotypical warrior's identity. Occasionally, in moments of high drama, for example when a soldier falls to the ground with a mortal wound, a Greek vase painter will depart from the usual convention of portraying his subject in profile, and offer us instead a front view (see fig. 102). The intention seems to be to force our attention through the helmet's disguise so that we focus on the pathos of the suffering victim. A similar effect is achieved by different means in the so-called

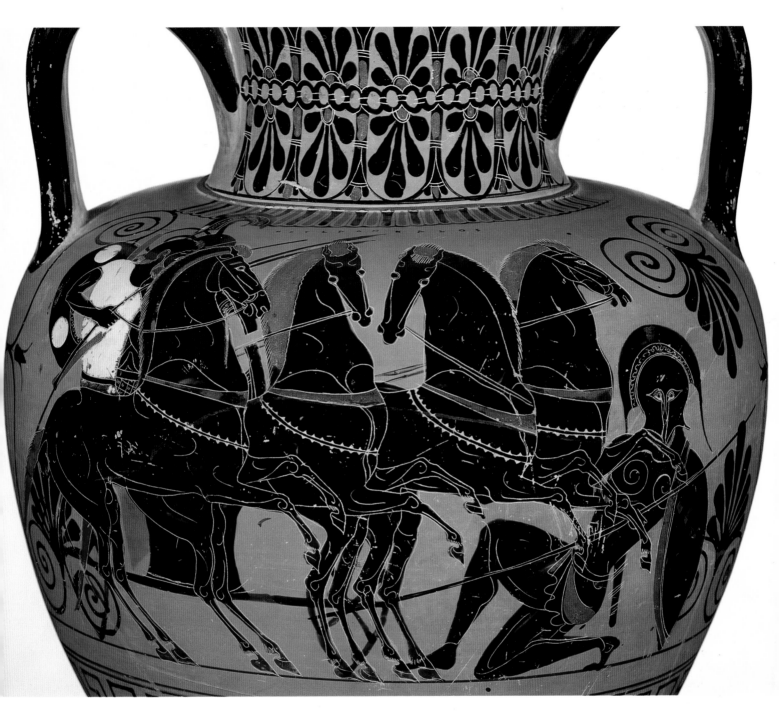

'Alexander Mosaic' showing Alexander the Great's defeat of the Persian king at the Battle of Issus (see fig. 103). In this mosaic from Pompeii, copied from a lost Hellenistic painting, we see one of the king's personal bodyguard, the so-called Immortals, fallen on the ground. Confronting the reality of death, he catches a glimpse of his own face, which is otherwise hidden from us, mirrored in a shield. The look of terror in the face of an Immortal would have been shocking enough, but the face of despair is supremely arresting and invites natural introspection.

103. Mosaic from the House of the Faun, Pompeii, probably copying an earlier Greek panel painting. There is a look of terror in the face of King Darius, as his defence buckles under the impact of Alexander's charge at the Battle of Issus. With wide eyes and gaping mouth, his is the expression of the tragic theatre mask. A different story is told by the figure in the bottom right of the picture. The Great King of Persia surrounded himself in battle with a bodyguard of so-called Immortals. One of the King's Immortals has fallen and, at the point of death, catches sight of his own reflection in the polished exterior of a bronze shield. We do not see the face itself, but we see his despair.

Another instance of the viewer's perception being directed through a mask is found in an extraordinary vase painting by Exekias, arguably the greatest exponent of the black-figure technique, showing Achilles in mortal combat with the Amazon queen Penthesilea (see fig. 104). This was no ordinary contest, for Achilles, the paragon of Greek aristocratic male values, is here pitched against a woman, albeit a warrior-queen. Achilles, dark and menacing, wears the Corinthian style of helmet, but his opponent, distinguished as a woman by the white of her flesh, wears the Athenian helmet-type, which leaves the face open. According to the story,

104. Scene from a black-figured *amphora* potted and painted by Exekias in Athens around 540–30 BC. Exekias was a peculiarly gifted painter in the black-figured technique, and his works often convey an intensity of feeling not found in other vase paintings of the same period. Here we see Achilles in combat with the Amazon queen, Penthesilea. Achilles wears the Corinthian form of the helmet, which masks the face. Penthesilea is shown with the Athenian type of helmet, where the face is left open. As Achilles plunges his spear into the Amazon's throat, she turns her gaze upon him. Her pitiful stare pierces Achilles' armour and, according to the story, he falls in love. H. of vase 41.5cm.

Achilles fell in love with his victim the very second he took her life. Exekias encapsulates the moment when the passions of love and death are experienced simultaneously: Achilles sinks his spear into Penthesilea's throat and, as the blood spurts, he catches sight of her beauty and falls in love. The contrasting characters of Achilles and Penthesilea are epitomised by their respective masks: the one is open, the other closed, but the pitiful glance of the victim pierces the external persona of her slayer and draws attention to the inner conflict of his soul.

Pathos is again evoked by the great literary unmasking of the Trojan prince Hector towards the end of Homer's *Iliad*. Leaving off fighting, Hector goes to meet his wife Andromache and son Astyanax, whom he finds waiting anxiously on the ramparts of the city. Homer touchingly describes how, as the hero draws near, the infant takes fright at the unaccustomed appearance of his father: only when the awesome helmet with its worrying crest is removed, does the child recognise him. Divested of his battle mask, Hector reveals a different face to his family, that of a tender husband and father confessing his secret fears.

Hector in a warrior's gear inspires terror in his impressionable son, who fails to see through the disguise and is forced to look away. The apotropaic effect of terrifying masks is brought out in the legend of the Gorgon, Medusa (see fig. 100): one look at the monster's face turned the spectator to stone. It was Perseus who contrived to decapitate Medusa by evading her literally petrifying gaze. The Gorgon, with her goggle eyes, protruding tongue and serpent-formed hair, became a kind of totem for the ancient Greeks and for the Athenians in particular. Athena, the divine protectress of their city, wore the Gorgon's head at the centre of her breastplate and it was woven into the robe that was dedicated to the goddess every four years on the Acropolis. The uncouth image with its uncompromising stare was worked into personal jewellery, emblazoned on battle shields and armour, set into the entablature of temples and painted on pottery. The Gorgon was by no means an Athenian preserve, and some of the earliest portrayals of her are found in a series of terracotta masks of the seventh century BC from the Spartan sanctuary of Artemis Orthia. Excavated from an ancient rubbish heap, they portray a variety of characters; as well as gorgons there are satyrs, youthful warriors, wrinkled old crones and other grotesques. Such terracotta masks were intended not for wearing, but rather as votive substitutes for actual masks worn in ritual dance at the shrine of Artemis. Real masks were made from such perishable materials as stiffened linen or wood and so have not survived.

Scholars of ancient theatre naturally locate the origins of later masked drama in the choral dances of the archaic period. At Athens the cult of Dionysos provided the ritual context out of which the classical theatre of the great tragedians and comic playwrights evolved. A chorus of masked dancers impersonating satyrs or animals occasionally appears on Athenian painted pottery of the sixth century BC. Even later, when drama developed speaking parts for actors, there was still a chorus of ten or so in every performance. Masks, then, were a part of Greek theatre long before the age of Aeschylus and Aristophanes, and we can happily discount the Greek tradition that attributed their invention to Thespis, the archetypal actor, from whom Thespians take their name. According to the story, Thespis gave the first performance of tragedy by disguising his face with white lead, before formalising this make-up in the wearing of true masks.

Our evidence for the theatre masks of the great fifth-century tragic play-wrights, Aeschylus, Sophocles and Euripides, is scanty and comes exclusively from vase paintings. Such as it is, it suggests that the mask covered more than just the face, being put on over the head like a helmet. The facial type was not, it seems, exaggerated in the manner of later Hellenistic and Roman theatre masks, but tended to present a somewhat blank expression, enlivened only by the gaping mouth through which the actor's voice had to be projected. These masks represented the general type of the character portrayed: beardless youth, bearded citizen, king, woman or god. In this, the theatre mask conformed with the convention of Greek sculpture and painting, where in the archaic and classical periods, the portrayal of individual personality was eschewed in favour of idealised form. The archaic freestanding male statue or *kouros*, with its formulaic features and artificial smile did not, intrinsically at least, portray any one person, but rather a type of person, namely aristocratic youth. The *kouros* was a sort of *tabula rasa* to which meaning could be attributed, depending on whether it was erected over a tomb or set up in a sanctuary, and on the nature of any message inscribed on the base or engraved on the figure itself. Context and inscription are to sculpture what drama and libretto are to the mask.

The word *drama* in ancient Greek comes from the verb 'to do' and literally means a deed; that is to say, an action represented upon the stage. The mask determined the basic persona of the actor which he would expand through the action and the narrative of the play. Tragic character was not, therefore, fixed and static, but the development of a tragic character frequently depended upon a reversal of fortune, which might necessitate an eventual change of mask, if the degree of transformation were such as to render the original mask redundant. Thus at the beginning of Sophocles's *Oedipus Tyrannus*, the hero is portrayed as a king at the height of his fame and fortune, but blind to the fact that he has killed his father and married his own mother. The play ends with his dreadful self-realisation, the agony of which causes him to put out his eyes. The act of mutilation takes place off-stage, and when the king re-emerges into the light, he is now masked as a blind beggar – sightless, but seeing what had previously been hidden from him.

Only in extreme reversals of fortune was such a change of mask necessary. Less violent changes of mood could be expressed by gesture alone, and by the movement of the head. Little is known for certain about the actual staging of Greek tragedy, but we may speculate that such techniques were used in the Greek theatre as are employed in Japanese Nō plays, where to lower the mask (*kumorasu*) is, literally, to 'cloud' it; while to look up (*terasu*) is to 'brighten' the mask. An illustration of how this might work in the Greek theatre may be found in the horsemen of the Parthenon frieze.

105. Scene from a red-figured *bell-krater* (wine-mixing bowl) made in Apulia (South Italy) around 380 BC. The comic actor's costume consisted of a skimpy tunic worn over a pair of tights, hung with a phallus of improbable proportions, often with a novel twist. The comic mask with its snub nose and rubbery lips was as outrageous as the costume. A bald slave is shown assisting the aged Centaur Chiron onto a stage building representing a healing sanctuary. Chiron has gone there to seek treatment for an arrow wound accidentally inflicted upon him by Herakles. The Centaur's mask parodies the features of a wise old man with heavy eyebrows and goatee beard. Centaurs are part-man, part-horse and Chiron's hind quarters are here personified by a second slave who is shown pushing from behind. H. of vase 37.5cm.

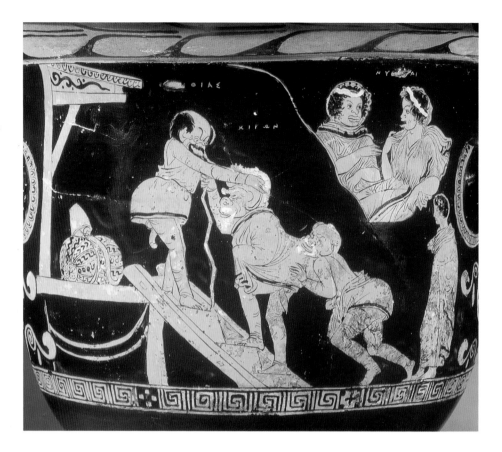

Here, according to the prevailing convention of Greek art, human figures in the cavalcade are represented as an idealised type: young men of aristocratic family, at an age for military service. From one to another the facial features of the horsemen are very similar, if not the same. A degree of variety in mood, however, is shown by the relative position in which the head is held. Thus some figures look straight ahead with a seeming air of self-assurance, while others appear more reflective with the face tilted down; a third group twist round to glance anxiously behind. The designer of the Parthenon frieze may have observed the expressive power of such varied deportment in the sign language of the theatre mask.

Such a comparison between the treatment of the face in architectural sculpture and that of the stage mask is particularly appropriate when we consider the distance at which both were viewed by the spectator. Whether standing at the foot of a temple looking up at a sculptured frieze, or sitting in the auditorium of a theatre looking down onto the players standing on the circular dance floor or *orchestra*, the facial image must be intelligible if it is to succeed. It was for practical, as well as formal reasons, therefore, that ancient theatre masks tended to present stereotypes, defining the general category of person to be portrayed, rather than particular personalities. This is true of both the tragic and comic theatre of all periods. There was, however, a period in Athenian drama when individual figures in public life were caricatured by their masks. The comic theatre of fifth-century Athens is known as Old Comedy to distinguish it from later so-called Middle and New Comedy. From what was undoubtedly the greatest period of Athenian theatre, only a few plays by Aristophanes survive entire. Aristophanes inhabited a society that was passionately interested in its own self-image and the principal figures who created it. This self-awareness on the part of the Athenian community afforded the comic playwright and the mask-makers scope to lampoon those who were, as we say, in the public eye. Thus Pericles was parodied in his own lifetime, as was Socrates, who is said during a performance of Aristophanes's *Clouds* to have stood up in the theatre so as to leave the audience in no doubt about the identity of the masked buffoon before them. Mask-makers were not necessarily free of reprisal from their victims, and in Aristophanes's *Knights* the poet explains how none would dare make a mask of the sinister demagogue Cleon.

The comic mask was worn with the loud costume of the comic actor (see fig. 105), which included a pair of tights hung with an oversize and often corkscrew phallus, invariably falling below the hem of a skimpy tunic. This, combined with the actor's absurd gestures, made the comic theatre the popular antithesis of noble tragedy.

One feature of both comedy and tragedy was the chorus of around ten

106. Scene from a black-figured amphora made in Athens around 540–30 BC. Archaic Greek vase painting sometimes depicted a type of choral song and dance, which seems to be the natural forerunner of Athenian drama of the fifth century BC. Aristophanes, the greatest Athenian comic playwright, won first prize at the Lenaea dramatic festival with his production of *Knights* in 424 BC. This, as the title suggests, had a chorus of horsemen, and in this vase painting we see just such a chorus performing over a century before Aristophanes's play was produced: three helmeted riders are shown mounted on a troop of dancers disguised as horses. H. of vase 33cm.

members, which, in the fifth century BC at least, was an integral part of the performance. Tragic choruses were usually human, but comedy allowed the mask-maker free range to exercise his imagination, and in Aristophanes alone we find choruses of Birds, Frogs, Wasps and even Clouds. We have already noted the animal choruses shown in some early representations predating the Aristophanic theatre: these seem to be the forerunners of Old Comedy (see fig. 106).

Another type of choric mask with a long history, one which finds a new theatrical context in the fifth century BC, was that worn by the satyrs (see fig. 107). The Greek imagination was populated with bogeymen, among them the lascivious satyrs, creatures part-man part-beast, who lived on wine and sex in the entourage of the god Dionysos. It became the custom for tragic playwrights to put on a satyr play, parodying some myth or

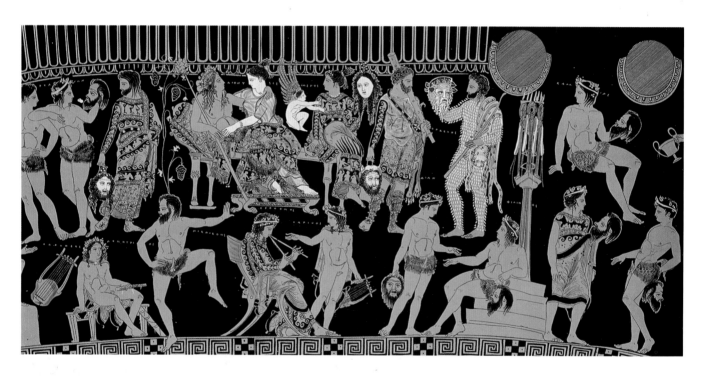

other, as light relief immediately following the performance of tragedy. Satyr plays served also to reinforce the Dionysiac element of dramatic performance, for it must always be remembered that the principal occasions for going to the theatre in ancient Athens were religious festivals dedicated to the god of wine. The theatre itself was situated in the god's sanctuary on the south slope of the Acropolis.

By the end of the fifth century BC the great age of Athenian drama was over and the classical world would never again see, except in repeat performance, the like of the tragic and comic genius of the Athenian playwrights. Masked theatre, however, was far from over and a wealth of monuments testify to the popularity in the later Greek and Roman periods of, in particular, comic authors such as Menander, Plautus and Terence. One of the striking features of later comedy is its tendency to standardise masks and so intensify the stereotyping of dramatic character. Julius Pollux, writing in the second century AD but drawing on earlier sources, lists six types of tragic mask for old men, eight for young men, three for different types of servant and eleven for women of all ages, in addition to those of such mythological characters as horned Actaeon, blind Phemius and other divine or heroic persons (see figs 108–111). These, and his lists of some forty-four comic masks, are of the greatest interest to students of the ancient theatre seeking names for the types of mask shown in numerous representations dating from the Graeco-Roman era.

Pollux makes frequent reference to the *onkos* as a feature of the tragic mask: by this he has in mind the raised forehead characteristic of some

108. Marble, Roman, first century BC or first century AD. Dramatic masks in the Hellenistic and Roman periods were reproduced in a variety of materials. This marble relief is perhaps copied from a Hellenistic mask portraying the 'Young Man' of New Comedy. H. 22.8cm.

109. (*right*) Terracotta from Myrina in Asia Minor, second century BC. The *pornoboskos* or pimp was one of the characters of New Comedy and his mask, with its long corkscrew square-cut beard and elaborate headgear, is one of the most distinctive. His head is heavily garlanded by a floral wreath worn over one of fruit and ivy leaves, while long streamers (partly broken) hang down to the shoulders on either side. H. 18.8cm.

110. Marble, Roman, first–second century AD. A miscreant slave seeking refuge from his master at an altar became one of the stock 'situations' of New Comedy. Sometimes he cups a hand to his ear as if mockingly to indicate that he has not heard his master's voice. This figure wears a mask with a broad beard and grinning mouth, through which we see the actor's own mouth. H. 61cm.

Graeco-Roman masks (see fig. 112). *Onkos* is a word used both in respect of masks, and to signify the elevated style of poetry raised above the level of everyday speech. It is one of the features that distinguishes the later tragic mask from the more understated mask of the earlier, fifth-century theatre. The onkos often goes together with an exaggerated expression of horror around the mouth and eyes, and is thought to have been introduced in the later fourth century BC, when the Athenian statesman Lycurgus rebuilt the theatre of Dionysos in stone. He equipped it with an architectural setting that threatened to dwarf the actors who aggrandised their appearance accordingly.

None of the masks that have come down to us from antiquity was ever worn in actual performance, but many may faithfully replicate the originals. A remarkable series of terracotta masks was found in votive deposits in the Sanctuary of Aeolus on the Italian island of Lipari. These, which must predate the Roman sack of the City of Lipari in 252 BC, remind us of the cache from the early Spartan Sanctuary of Artemis Orthia and testify to the continued religious significance of masks. There is, however, a parallel tendency in the later Greek and Roman periods to exploit the obvious

111. Terracotta made on Melos around 300–275 BC. Slaves, divided into various categories, were among the stock characters of New Comedy. The mask shown here with a fierce expression and grizzled beard is wreathed for participation in a festival. H. 100.2cm.

113. Graeco-Roman, second–first century BC. This striking mask was once fitted to the handle of a bronze *situla* (bucket). It appears to represent the Greek god Dionysos in a cult form probably invented in Egypt under the rule of the Ptolemies. The bronze is enhanced with inlays in other metals: iron for the ribbon around the forehead, silver for the eyes and copper for the ivy berries and lips. In addition the mask displays two pairs of horns: a small goatish horn inlaid with copper is worked into the hair at the temples, while a more prominent pair of silver horns spring from holes cast into either side of the forehead. H. 21.4cm.

decorative effect of the mask for purely secular purposes. Masks, and particularly those of Dionysos and his followers, are used again and again in all manner of plastic and graphic ornament: as models in terracotta, bronze or marble, engraved on gemstones, painted into frescoes, or worked into mosaic (see figs 113, 115). It must always be remembered, however, in defining the meaning of such images, that in the ancient world the line between sacred and secular was thinly drawn, if at all. Even in seemingly mundane contexts such as a garden wall or courtyard floor, a mask may have evoked the householder's religious beliefs as well as his cultural pretensions.

Many masks, no doubt, carried more than one meaning; thus, on sarcophagi of the Roman imperial period, dramatic masks were often set at the corners of the coffin-lid or shown in representations of the deceased. These are not, usually at least, an indication that the occupant of the sarcophagus was an actor or poet in life; but he may have wished it to be known that he was a *mousikos aner*, that is to say, someone who was literate in the musical, literary and philosophical arts, or, at the very least, that he was a theatre-goer (see fig. 114). Alternatively, the mask with its tragic grimace may be apotropaic, to ward off the evil eye; or again, it may signify a Dionysiac element in the deceased's beliefs about the afterlife, or it may express a morbid sentiment about the tragedy of death. As often in trying to interpret the past, it is as well to keep an open mind.

112. Marble relief, Roman, first or second century AD. Contrary to popular belief, the masks of the tragic theatre of the fifth century BC were not horrific, but tended to present a blank, if serious expression. As stage buildings became bigger and more elaborate, however, the actor was required to appear more conspicuous, so as not to be dwarfed by the grandiose setting. This type of mask with wide staring eyes and gaping, seemingly screaming, mouth belongs to the later Hellenistic and Roman periods. A notable feature is the high forehead that added height to the actor's stature. H. 17.8cm.

114. Marble, Roman, about AD 270–300. Part of the lid of the sarcophagus of Marcus Sempronius Nicocrates. The deceased is shown communing with a muse who leans on a pillar beside him. A tragic mask is prominently displayed in both sculpted panels and in the central panel an inscription in Greek explains the significance: it begins 'M. Sempronius Nicocrates', and then goes on to explain how he was once a *mousikos aner*, which in this case means more than just someone of Greek cultivated taste, for he was literally a poet and musician. Latterly, the epigram explains, he gave up his musical career for the less tiring life of a pimp. Ultimately, however, 'in death the muses take possession of my body'. L. 116.6cm.

One distinctively Roman tradition in the funerary use of masks was the ritual involving death masks. When a male member of one of the patrician families died, an impression of his face was taken in wax and was worn in the funerary cortège by another, who had practised imitating the dead person while he was alive. Others would wear the masks of the deceased's ancestors. After the ceremony these masks were kept in an open cupboard in the house. Related to this practice is the peculiar truth to life of early Roman portrait sculpture. The Romans embraced realism in portraiture where the Greeks had tended to shun it. Lifelike reproduction of facial features was associated in Roman custom with the right to a death mask as a mark of noble birth that underscored the importance of lineage (see fig. 116). To a Greek the idea of accurate reproduction of a face had little appeal until the Roman era.

Mask and face in classical antiquity may, as I have attempted to show, be profitably studied together. It is axiomatic of our understanding that we abandon all modern notions of the one representing a higher reality or a greater truth than the other. The purpose of the mask in antiquity was not, as is so often taken today, to deceive. The classical mask has become the abiding symbol of theatre in the West, where the grimace of tragedy and the leer of comedy are to be found on every performance programme. This is ironic when we consider that, with rare exceptions, masked drama is largely eschewed by the modern European stage. When a mask does make a fleeting appearance, it is usually a disguise for a figure whose real identity will be revealed as the plot unfolds. Indeed, the general impression we have of masks – in the theatre, at a masked ball, at such festivals as Halloween – is of something sinister or clandestine. Our natural impulse when confronted by a mask is to ask what it conceals. The key to understanding the role of the mask in the ancient world is not to pose this question, but to take it at face value.

115. Sard, Roman, first century BC–first century AD. The decorative appeal of tragic masks was exploited by every variety of art. This mask of a youthful Dionysos wreathed with ivy is cut into a semi-precious sealstone. 13 × 12mm.

116. Marble, Roman, first century
BC. A Roman patrician carrying the
portrait busts of his ancestors.
Roman sculptors developed the art of
portraiture to a degree of verism not
seen before. Busts of ancestors were
kept in the house and when a
leading member of one of the noble
families died, a wax model was cast
from his death mask to be worn by
a person impersonating him at the
funeral. This statue portrays a
patrician carrying busts of his
ancestors in a funeral procession.
His grave expression suggests an
epitome of traditional Roman values.

MASKS IN ANCIENT EGYPT
THE IMAGE OF DIVINITY

117. Painted wooden mummy mask, datable on stylistic grounds to the later Eighteenth Dynasty, about 1350 BC. It was probably made for a woman. The front and back were carved from separate pieces of sycamore fig and joined together. The exterior was then plastered and painted, the interior being left rough. Piercings in the ear-lobes are represented in paint. Two holes in the lower front edge and one at the back perhaps served to accommodate cords used to secure the mask to the mummy. At this period, the use of a mask was optional and seems to have been provided only in the burials of persons of some wealth and status. H. 43.5cm.

118. Cartonnage mask on the mummy of a man named Ankhef, from Asyut, about 1950 BC. The yellow colouring of the face denotes the deceased's newly acquired status as a divine being, with shining golden flesh, and is used in lieu of the more expensive gold leaf. These early masks were placed over the head while the wrapping of the mummy was still in progress. They were secured with linen thongs and then further wrappings were applied, covering the flaps of the mask and holding it in place. The damage to the side of the face is probably the result of the body having been laid on its left side with the head supported by a wooden headrest – the customary method of burial in the Middle Kingdom, done in order to bring the mummy's face into alignment with the eyes painted on the eastern-facing side of the coffin. H. 50cm.

All true ancient Egyptian masks were made to serve a religious purpose. Disguise or concealment of the features was not an aim; rather the mask was a medium for the elevation of the wearer to the level of divinity, a role which applies as much to the animal masks occasionally worn by the living, as to the funerary headpieces placed on the mummified bodies of the dead. A means of personal access to divine qualities was felt to be important when confronted by situations which required more than ordinary human abilities to deal with – in life, the threat of illness and the danger of accident; after death, the hazardous passage into the afterlife.

According to the concept of sympathetic magic, the putting on of a mask identified the wearer with another entity – usually one connected with the realm of the supernatural. It conferred superhuman abilities, particularly the power to ward off danger of various kinds. Because of this belief, it appears likely that the mask had a role to play in Egyptian cult and magical practices, where the main protagonists were often identified with deities. Unfortunately, evidence for the use of masks in this context is rather meagre; they would probably have been made of perishable materials, leaving few traces in the archaeological record. Artistic depictions of humans with animal heads performing rituals are highly ambiguous, for how are we to tell whether such events are supposed to be happening in the divine sphere, with the gods themselves participating directly, or on earth with priests acting out the roles of those gods? If the latter, does the iconography of the animal-headed figure simply serve to identify the god in question, or is it to be taken more literally as a depiction of a priest wearing a mask? Inscriptions provide little help, and the problem is further complicated by the fact that the ancient Egyptian language possessed no specific term for 'mask'.

Nonetheless, there is some evidence for the use of masks in rituals aimed at curing the illnesses and accidents of everyday life. In the ruins of a house at Kahun, Flinders Petrie found a full-sized grotesque mask made of painted cartonnage, with eye-holes to enable the wearer to see. It probably represents a lion-demon, such as Bes or Aha, and may have been worn by a magician during the performance of apotropaic rituals. A wooden statuette, found in a tomb near the Ramesseum at Thebes, represents a woman apparently wearing such a mask and grasping the snake wands which seem to have been part of the magician's equipment. The Kahun mask and the statuette date to the nineteenth and eighteenth centuries BC but animal masks may well have been worn at other periods; the scarcity of evidence is probably partly a reflection of the fact that the rites in which they were used were a feature of religious life among the peasants, about which we are less well-informed than about the rituals performed in the main cult-temples.

More debatable is the often-repeated statement that masks were worn

119. This fine mummy mask, made for a woman, depicts the deceased wearing a striped wig and the winged vulture-headdress. It was constructed of painted and gilded cartonnage shaped over a mould, the negative impression of which is visible on the interior. The inscriptions below the collar are standard invocations requesting offerings and a good burial for the owner. The mask was formerly attributed to the Middle Kingdom but recent research suggests that it actually dates to the early Eighteenth Dynasty. Pieces of inscribed linen in the British Museum, which evidently come from the same burial, give the dead lady's name as Satdjehuty and add that she was an honoured contemporary of Queen Ahmose-Nefertary, wife of Ahmose I. Her status as a royal favourite might also explain the high quality of the mask and the inclusion of the vulture-headdress, exceptional for a non-royal person. H. 52cm.

120. Mask from the mummy of the lady Henutmehit from Thebes, Nineteenth or Twentieth Dynasty (*c*.1295–1069 BC). It is made of cedarwood, plastered, painted and gilded. Unlike earlier masks, this one included the crossed arms of the dead lady. A mummy-shaped cover of gilded wood, with scenes in openwork showing the deceased before the gods of the Underworld, was placed over the abdomen and legs. The two halves together comprised a mummy-board, placed directly over the wrapped body in its coffin. H. 70cm.

by priests during funerary rituals to impersonate Anubis, the god responsible for the embalming of the deceased. At first glance the evidence appears substantial: beginning in the fifteenth century BC, hundreds of paintings on the walls of tombs, on papyri and on coffins show a jackal-headed male figure performing the last rites on the mummy, often in association with priests and mourners, and a sketch of a burial, on an ostracon, shows a jackal-headed figure apparently receiving the mummy into its tomb. A painted pottery jackal-mask with eye- or air-holes under the snout, in the Hildesheim Museum, has often been adduced as 'proof' that such headpieces were used in these ceremonies, yet its weight (8kg) and the small apertures for the shoulders make it a strangely impracticable piece of headgear. Written references to the wearing of jackal-masks are not found before the Classical era, when they are known to have been used in the rituals of the Hellenistic Isis cult. The only unequivocal pictorial evidence also comes from the Roman period: in a procession of priests depicted on a wall of the temple of Dendera is a man with a jackal-mask placed over his head (his face visible within it) and apparently unable to see clearly, since one of his fellows is guiding his footsteps. While this scene may indicate that such masks were used in Roman Egypt, it cannot automatically be assumed that the earlier depictions of jackal-headed humans testify to their use in the Pharaonic period. The Dendera relief may represent nothing more than an attempt to explain the puzzling jackal-headed figures in Pharaonic art, at a time when their original significance was no longer understood. It may be that the New Kingdom depictions of the jackal-headed man were meant to convey the idea of the god's direct participation in the funeral rituals – in other words, that they represent Anubis himself, not a priest impersonating him.

One further context in which masks representing the gods might have been worn is during the religious 'dramas' which were performed at some temples on festival days. It would be logical to suppose that the actors taking the parts of Horus or Thoth might have put on falcon- or ibis-masks, respectively. Here too, however, special costumes may not have been considered essential to the actors' adoption of their roles; the women who played the parts of Isis and Nephthys were identified simply by having the names of the deities written on their arms.

If the wearing of masks by the living is frustratingly difficult to demonstrate, their inclusion among funerary equipment is easier to account for. The masks placed over the heads of mummies almost invariably reproduce the features of the human face. They represent the deceased in the divine state which he or she aspired to attain after death – identified with a variety of deities, but chiefly with Osiris and the sun-god, the main agents of resurrection. The majority of mummy masks were mass-produced, with stereotyped features; only in the case of specially-commissioned pieces for

121. (left and opposite) Mummy mask of Hornedjitef from Thebes. The official titles inscribed on Hornedjitef's coffins indicate that he lived under Ptolemy III (246–222 BC). His mask is made of layers of linen with a thin outer coating of plaster, painted and gilded, with the details of the collar, necklace and inscribed headband in slightly raised relief. On the crown of the head is a complex scene symbolising rebirth: the solar disc is pushed up by the winged scarab beetle, which is itself supported by a representation of Osiris, ruler of the terrestrial Underworld, in the form of his emblem, a Djed pillar equipped with human attributes. Isis, Nephthys and other divinities appear to left and right, and below is the goddess Hathor in the form of a cow. At each side a falcon, representing Horus, protects with his wings the name of Osiris written in a cartouche. The inscription around the brows is a version of the ancient 'spell for the mysterious head', in which the parts of the deceased's head are identified with the members of various gods. H. 38cm.

122. (right) This mummy of a priest named Irthorru, buried at Akhmim, about 600 BC, is unusual for its period in having been provided with a fine gilded mask of natural size. This is one of the earliest non-royal masks to have a curled 'divine' beard. The technique of construction is also unusual, for the mask appears to form an integral part with the mummy wrappings. The face was perhaps modelled separately and then attached to the mummy on a foundation of resinous material, which formed the basis for the shaping of the wig. H. 36cm.

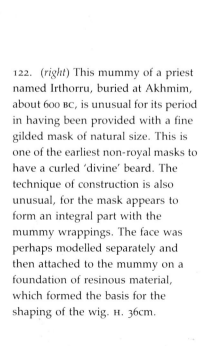

royal persons, such as the gold mask of Tutankhamun, can any attempt at capturing a likeness be detected. It was in fact the norm for images of the deceased, whether tomb statues, anthropoid coffins or mummy masks, to be idealised, and this did not hinder their magical efficacy as substitutes for the corpse – they were deputies which could provide the spirit with the physical form necessary for survival, in case the actual body should perish. Significantly, one of the worst disasters which the Egyptians feared in the next world was the loss of the head. Chapter 43 of the Book of the Dead, the 'Spell for preventing a man's decapitation in the realm of the dead', stresses 'The head of Osiris shall not be taken from him; my head shall not be taken from me.' The mask, acting as a substitute for the head, provided security in the event of such a loss, but this was not its only function. Other inscriptions, to be discussed below, reveal that mummy masks also had more specific roles to play in the Egyptians' efforts to guarantee the continued survival of the spirit after death.

The first true mummy masks appeared in the twenty-second or twenty-first century BC (see fig. 118), but their precursors can be recognised in burials dating back to the Old Kingdom (about 2686–2181 BC). Already at this period special attention was being devoted to the head; the painting of the facial features on the mummy wrappings or the modelling of them in white plaster directly over the bandages (a treatment sometimes applied to the entire body in the Fifth and Sixth Dynasties) were formative stages in the tradition which was to culminate in the development of separately-made mummy masks, covering the head and shoulders of the corpse. These masks have been found in burials of the First Intermediate Period and Middle Kingdom (c.2181–1650 BC) at sites throughout Egypt, and as far afield as Mirgissa in Nubia. Some were made of wood but the majority were of cartonnage – a lightweight and versatile material made from layers of linen, stuccoed inside and out. The face and headdress were fashioned on a mould, and small details such as ears were separately made of wood or clay and attached afterwards. The deceased was represented wearing a tripartite wig, sometimes striped or overlaid with a winged headdress. Blue was the most usual colour for wigs both on masks and coffins; it probably imitated the blue lapis lazuli of which the hair of divine beings was supposed to be made. The face was painted yellow or red, or gilded. Eyes were sometimes inlaid: a mask from the tomb of Djehutynakht at Bersha (Eleventh Dynasty, c.2125–1985 BC) had eyes of ivory in copper settings. Many masks prepared for men had a painted beard and moustache. A fillet frequently encircled the wig and an amuletic collar was represented on the breast. At this period the mask usually terminated in large flaps which passed over the shoulders and covered the chest and back. In the burials of women the bare breasts were sometimes depicted on this section – an example found at Asyut has the breasts modelled in the round.

123. Gilded cartonnage mask of the Ptolemaic period, found on a mummy excavated at Atfih, opposite the Faiyum, in 1911. This site produced many undisturbed mummies with cartonnage masks, footcases and body ornaments. This example exhibits constructional and decorative techniques common to many masks of the Ptolemaic period. The face has been pressed out from the inside using a mould which, in this instance, has produced vague, indistinct features; the negative impression of the mould can be seen on the inside. The ears, lacking all anatomical detail, and the large painted eyes resembling hieroglyphic signs, contribute to the bland, unrealistic impression. H. 41cm.

Some of these early masks carry an inscription which throws additional light on their function. It is found, as Spell 531, in the great collection of religious literature known as the Coffin Texts, and in the New Kingdom a revised version of it was incorporated in the Book of the Dead (chapter 151B). In its later form this 'Spell for the mysterious head' addresses the mask: 'Hail to you whose face is kindly, Lord of vision . . . kindly face who is among the gods!' It goes on to identify the individual parts of the mask with the appropriate members of different deities or with the barques in which the sun-god travelled – carriers of the potential for resurrection: 'Your right eye is the Night-barque, your left eye is the Day-barque, your eyebrows are (those of) the Ennead (the nine gods of the Heliopolitan creation story), your forehead is (that of) Anubis, the nape of your neck is (that of) Horus, your locks of hair are (those of) Ptah-Sokar . . .' A version of the text is inscribed on the gold mask of Tutankhamun, where it continues: 'You are in front of the Osiris, he sees thanks to you, you guide him on good roads, you smite for him the confederates of Seth so

124. The facial features of mummy masks from the Ptolemaic period were often highly stylised – reproduced mechanically by painters without any feeling for the unity of the whole. This example from Sedment is typical of this tendency. The beard-straps on the sides of the face, depicted as a discreet narrow line on some early Ptolemaic masks (cf. fig. 121) have here been expanded into thick bands covering the cheeks. The grotesque impression is compounded by the unusual depiction of the mouth, with the lips drawn back and the front teeth bared in a hideous smile. H. 35.5cm.

that he may overthrow your enemies before the Ennead of the Gods . . .' Through this last reference the deceased is identified with Osiris, who was murdered by his brother Seth and resurrected, the god who above all others was the key to rebirth. But this is not all; the description of the mask as the 'mysterious head' points to an identification of it in the minds of the Egyptians with the head of the sun-god, who, as he journeyed through the Underworld by night, illuminated the subterranean caverns with his shining golden face, and brought new life to the dead who dwelt there. The mask thus provided the deceased with the necessities for a safe passage into the afterlife – not merely the blue hair, collar and golden flesh of a divine being, but the physical attributes of a whole range of specific gods. It identified him simultaneously with Osiris and Re, the sun-god – a double assurance of resurrection.

The mummy masks of the Middle Kingdom marked the beginning of a long tradition which was to continue, in spite of interruptions, until the fourth century AD. They also had a major influence – technically and iconographically – on the development of the anthropoid coffin. Early mummiform coffins have the appearance of being extensions of the mask, sharing the same constructional methods and having similar decoration. Throughout the succeeding centuries the function of masks and mummiform coffins remained closely linked.

Masks of wood, cartonnage and metal are attested in many burials of the New Kingdom (about 1550–1069 BC) (see figs 117, 119). That of Tutankhamun is the finest, but masks made for high-ranking courtiers were also accomplished works of art – a fine example is that of Tjuyu, mother of Queen Tiye, in the Cairo Museum. They were provided for children as well as adults, and small masks were sometimes placed on the embalmed viscera of the deceased, which were prepared for burial as if they were miniature human bodies. During this period the magical role of mummy masks and anthropoid coffins grew closer and overlapped, and by the thirteenth century BC the use of a separate mask was giving way – at least at Thebes – to the provision of a mummy board, a kind of extra coffin lid placed over the body (see fig. 120).

For about nine hundred years (1200–300 BC) the anthropoid coffin, incorporating an idealised face of the deceased, was predominant in Egyptian burials, and the mummy mask as a separate entity was used only occasionally. Among the very few examples datable to this period are the spectacular gold masks of the kings of the Twenty-first and Twenty-second Dynasties, buried at Tanis in the Delta. They are clearly based on New Kingdom models. A brief revival of the tradition can be dated to the Twenty-sixth Dynasty (664–525 BC) (see fig. 114), when high officials buried at Saqqara and Hawara in the Faiyum, were provided with small masks of gold or silver, incorporated into bead-nets placed over the outer mummy wrappings. This phenomenon is also encountered far to the south of Egypt in the royal cemeteries of the Kushites at Nuri and Meroe.

The final great flowering of the mummy mask tradition in Egypt began under the Ptolemaic rulers (305–30 BC) and continued through the centuries of Roman rule. Cartonnage masks were a regular feature of burials in the Ptolemaic period, when they were usually associated with footcases and body-plaques of the same material. The masks belong firmly in the pharaonic tradition, with tripartite wig, fillet, collar, and painted or gilded face. The sides, back and top were decorated with figures of deities or religious scenes evoking the perennial theme of rebirth (see fig. 121). Layers of linen were usually shaped over a mould to create the face, yet the features are frequently indistinct; more importance seems to have been attached to the gilding of the surface and the painting of the wig in bright colours (see figs 12 in Introduction, 123, 124).

The impact of the Roman conquest of Egypt is clearly reflected in the development of mummy masks, which exhibit a progressive fusing of

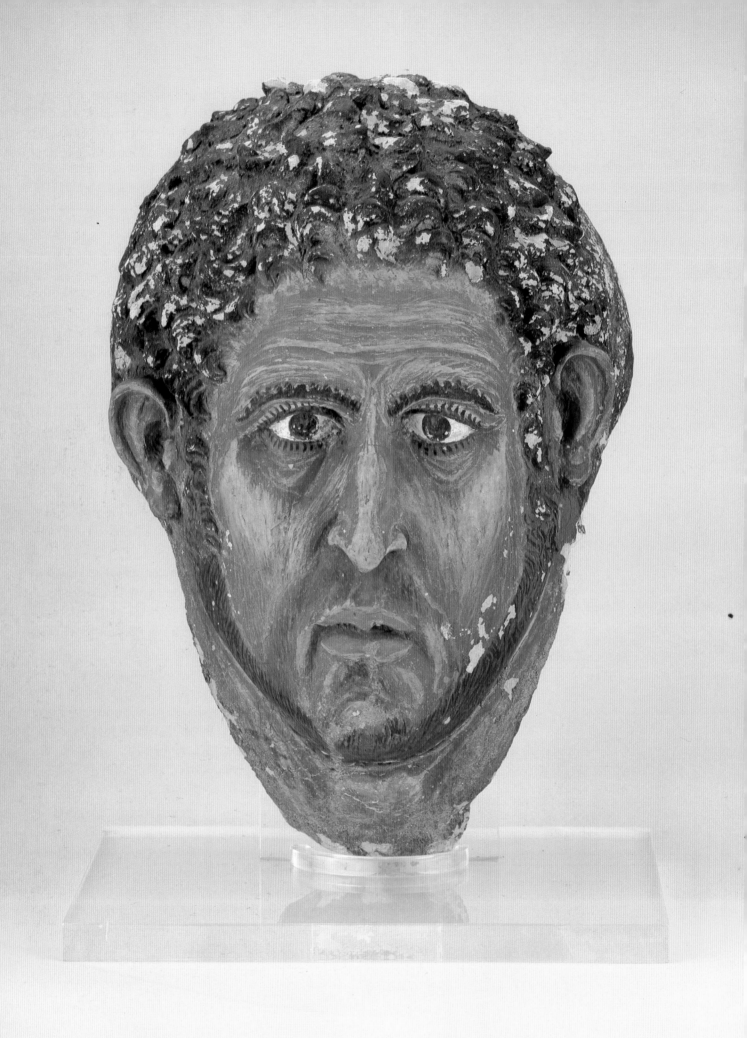

pharaonic traditions with elements inspired by the art and fashions of the Mediterranean world. Whereas the faces of Ptolemaic masks were bland and without individuality, the trend in the Roman period was increasingly towards realism. The custom of providing an eternal image of the deceased encompassed the well-known 'encaustic' (wax-painted) panel portraits from the Faiyum area, and paintings on linen shrouds, as well as three-dimensional masks in a variety of forms. The placing of these on the mummy was a continuation of the Egyptian tradition through which the mask acted as a substitute head and, by magical means, provided the

125. (*opposite*) The commonest type of mummy mask from the Roman period was the painted plaster head. This example found on the mummy of a man excavated at Hu (Diospolis Parva) in Upper Egypt, dates to the first century AD, and is an early example of the type. It is hollowed out behind to enable it to be fitted directly over the mummy's head. Whereas the majority of the plaster heads were made in moulds, this one was individually modelled by hand, making it one of the most lifelike examples known. H. 27cm.

126. Mould-made plaster mask of a woman, probably from Meir in Middle Egypt, and dating to the second century AD. Roman period masks from Meir usually show the deceased wearing a *chiton*; here the breast, with details of the woman's dress, has been broken away. The hair is arranged in a triple row of short curls on the forehead, with longer ones passing behind the ears. Earrings and a necklace are modelled in the round, and a wreath surmounts the head. H. 35cm.

183 · THE IMAGE OF DIVINITY

127. Alongside the plaster heads and the 'encaustic' panel portraits of the Roman period, the pharaonic tradition of cartonnage masks continued. This example, made for a person named Syros, comes from a family-group of mummies found at Hawara, and perhaps dates to the late first century AD. Its shape and the paintings of Egyptian deities are in the Ptolemaic tradition. These include Ba birds, winged serpents and sphinxes, the sky-goddess Nut and scenes of the deceased, as a mummy and offering to the gods. The face, probably fashioned over a mould, projects from the surrounding headdress and is more realistic than those of Ptolemaic masks. The eyes are elaborately made according to a method characteristic of Roman period masks from the Faiyum area: the whites are of crystalline limestone with separate irises and pupils of differently coloured glass. The name of the owner is written in Greek on the top of the head. H. 49.5cm.

128. Roman period cartonnage mask from the Faiyum area, probably Hawara. It completely enveloped the head of the mummy, and would originally have extended to the waist at the front. It probably dates to the first century AD, and in its style shows a characteristic mixture of pharaonic and Hellenistic elements. The gilded face is purely classical. Framing the face is a winged scarab beetle and figures of Egyptian deities in raised relief, while the sides, back and top of the head have painted depictions of traditional Egyptian funerary motifs. The inlaid eyes are set in copper-alloy sockets, serrated along their outer edges to imitate eyelashes. H. 30.5cm.

deceased with the power to be resurrected, an intention further perpetuated through the images and texts relating to rebirth and transfiguration, painted on the sides and back of the mask (see fig. 128). The realism of the actual heads derives, however, from the world of Roman art, as does the representation of the deceased dressed in the fine clothes, jewellery and hair styles of daily life – symbols of the earthly existence which it was hoped would continue after death. During the first three centuries AD the masks show many varied responses to the artistic challenge of blending the iconography of these traditions.

The commonest mummy portraits used during the Roman period were the three-dimensional and strikingly realistic plaster heads found mainly in Middle Egypt (notably Hermopolis Magna and Antinoopolis) and in the area around Alexandria – a wonderfully rich gallery of Roman faces adorned with all the variations of hairstyle and jewellery made fashionable by the imperial families (see figs 125, 126, 129–133). Yet despite the initial impression of naturalism which the masks create, they are not depictions of real individuals, for when large numbers are compared it becomes apparent that they are stereotypes (young man, bearded man, mature woman, and so on) and they were clearly mass-produced. The basic head was usually cast in a mould, from which it emerged without eyes or ears, and for the most part without details of hair or jewellery. These features were added separately, the details of hair, beard and ornaments being modelled

130. Plaster mask, probably from Hermopolis West, dating to around 200 AD, one of a group which represents the final stage in the evolution of this type – the head fully modelled in the round and raised up at right angles to the body, with the garment depicted and the hands represented as if lying on the breast. The eyes are inlaid according to a method introduced about the time of Hadrian, in which the eyeball is covered by a plate of transparent glass. H. 28.5cm.

with a spatula or knife. Variations in the finish of the mask apparently depended on the amount the purchaser wished to spend: the surface could be either painted or gilded (see fig. 133), and the eyes simply modelled in plaster and inserted into the sockets, or carefully constructed from crystal-line limestone, with pupils of obsidian or coloured glass and lids of bronze with disturbingly realistic eyelashes (see figs 127–128).

The plaster masks seem to have fallen out of use after the third century AD. In the fourth century, burial customs in Egypt changed dramatically, and mummification, with the associated adornment of the body, was abandoned. Some painted linen mummy covers with stucco faces from Thebes, dating to the early fourth century, are perhaps among the latest examples of the tradition – their features, typical of late Roman art, already foreshadow Coptic painting styles.

Other products of Egyptian craftsmen which might be – and sometimes are – described as masks, have not been touched on here. These include

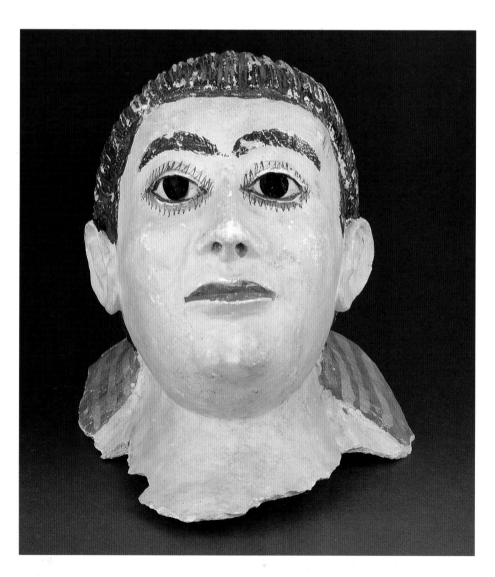

129. During the second century AD the development of the plaster masks led to the emergence of a type in which the whole of the head, including the back, was realistically modelled in the round. This example, perhaps from Hermopolis West, is thought to date to about the period of the emperor Trajan (98–117 AD). It illustrates an early stage in the development, showing the deceased with his head resting on a kind of pillow. Only the upper part of the back of the head is modelled in the round. H. 20.5cm.

the famous sculptors' prototypes from Amarna (often, but inaccurately, termed 'masks'), and the frontal depictions of the head of Hathor, sometimes used as a repeating motif in tomb friezes or as column capitals; they are 'masks' only to the extent that this goddess was one of the few deities

131. Plaster head of a bearded man, about 200 AD. The shoulders and breast have been broken away, and much of the paint has been lost. The inlaid eyes are covered with a plate of transparent glass, and on the back of the neck are traces of a painted scene of lamentation over the dead body. H. 26.5cm.

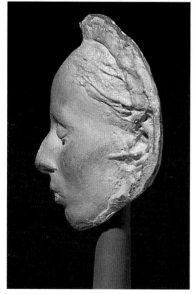

132. (*left*) The only authentic example of a death mask from ancient Egypt is a plaster mould found at Saqqara in 1907–8, in the funerary temple attached to the pyramid of King Teti (Sixth Dynasty, about 2345–2181 BC). Casts taken from this mould show a face with relaxed muscles and collapsed features, indicating that the subject was a dead person. The excavators assumed that the face was that of Teti himself or his wife, and that the mask may have been used as a model for sculptors carving statues to be installed in the temple. This explanation, however, is inconsistent with what is known of the production of statuary in pharaonic Egypt. Classical sources, however, indicate that death masks were made to be carried in the funeral processions of members of Roman patrician families (they may even have served as models for naturalistic sculptures) and it is possible that the Saqqara example belongs to this period, particularly as the area of Teti's pyramid was used extensively as a cemetery for private individuals in the Graeco-Roman period. H. 21cm.

to be regularly depicted full-face in Egyptian art and her image was often used in tombs or on objects to confer the protection or promote the assistance of the goddess. It is possible that the Roman custom of making 'death masks' was also adopted in Egypt in the early centuries AD, but how

133. Gilded mask of a young man, wearing a wreath and a medallion. This plaster head is dated to the early third century AD; the arrangement of the hair like a close-fitting cap is characteristic of the reign of the emperor Alexander Severus. Variations in hairstyles and jewellery are important clues to the dating of Roman plaster heads and encaustic panel portraits from Egypt. Thanks to the rapid dissemination throughout the Roman empire of portraits of emperors and empresses, their distinctive hairstyles could be – and were – copied on mummy portraits after only a short interval. H. 24cm.

common this was cannot be determined on account of the sparsity of the evidence – one example alone has been identified, and that of uncertain date (see fig. 132).

The aim of those items which may be truly called masks was essentially the transfiguration of the wearer – to enable him or her to harness divine power and to manipulate it for practical ends. When placed on a mummy, the mask focused on to the deceased divine attributes and associations crucial to a successful passage into the afterlife, recreating him on a new, higher plane of existence. Hence with funerary masks, as with so many of the products of ancient Egyptian craftsmen, the motivation to triumph over death and decay led to the creation of some of the greatest surviving works of ancient art.

THE OTHER WITHIN

MASKS AND MASQUERADES IN EUROPE

Controversy and questions

European masks and masquerading have recently been placed by Ginzburg right at the centre of a web of practices and beliefs involving witchcraft, the persecution of Jews and lepers, spirit possession and shamanism, the dead and the other world. In particular, animal masks have been located within a network of beliefs concerning travels to the land of the dead in ritual contexts of renewal and fertility. The implications of this study are far-reaching, even if its historical span, although including the Christian era, stops at the Renaissance.

One element is of special interest here. The dominant trend in the contemporary study of masks moves in the opposite direction to the ideas of nineteenth- and early twentieth-century folklorists. They variously held that masking and other folk practices were to be considered 'survivals'

134. A *Wüescht Chläus* (Ugly Chläus) from Urnäsch (Canton Appenzell, Switzerland). See fig. 139.

135. Moena (Dolomites, Italy). Two *Arlechign* (Harlequins) chasing children during the 1980 Carnival.

of pre-Christian, 'primitive' and 'pagan' cultural systems. It was only by postulating the existence of a coherent foundation of ancient beliefs concerning magic and fertility, the spirits of the wild or the destiny of the dead, that the meaning and function of masquerading could be clarified. Modern anthropological studies, however, have been inclined to make sense of European masking practices in terms of the fully-documented sociological and symbolic contexts in which they occur. Thus, for the most part, even those contemporary masquerades for which early documentation is available do not now retain any coherent set of supporting 'beliefs'. If a masquerader of a Tyrolean village is asked why he is donning, say, a *Schiachtpercht* mask, he will be most unlikely to reply that his actions help the crops to grow strong and healthy. Ginzburg, however, has reopened the issue. He seeks to demonstrate that below the surface of dominant European culture a current of implicit beliefs, expressed in practices incompatible with the dominant religious tenets and related ultimately

to pre-Christian ideas, did persist. They may never have been formalised in any coherent doctrinal corpus or uttered as an explicit 'creed'. However, the connection between masking, the celebration of the dead and hazy, complex notions of 'witches' and 'spirits' (to mention one theme among others), creeps through the tightest mesh of official cultural politics and keeps coming back, its echoes reaching into contemporary times and attesting the presence of 'the Other' within modern European culture.

Let us consider some examples.

THE WILD HUNT

A chapter of the *Historia Ecclesiastica* of Orderic Vitalis, written in about 1140, reports the extraordinary adventure of the priest Walchelin of St Aubin de Bonneval. On the night of 1 January 1091, as he was walking home along a path, he heard a great, clanging noise similar to that of an army on the move. He saw marching past a giant armed with a cudgel, followed by a multitude of men and women, all undergoing some kind of torment. Among them he could easily distinguish clerics, women of pleasure, soldiers and knights. He was witnessing the march of the *Familia Herlechini*. In Walchelin's interpretation of the vision, the followers of the giant were the souls of Purgatory expiating their sins.

This is one of the earliest literary records of the Christianisation of a myth diffused in the popular cultures of Europe. What is variously known as the Wild Hunt, *Wilde Jagde*, *Caccia Selvaggia* and similar names, is the procession of the dead wandering about on certain nights of the year. The leaders of the 'hunt' were characters associated with the underworld in the pagan foundation of European culture, such as *Perchta*, *Holda*, *Hera*, *Diana*, *Erodiana/Erodiade/Redodesa*, *Hecates*, *Hellequin*, *Harlequin* or *Harlechinus* (from 'hell', the underworld in Anglo-Saxon languages) as well as various other local variations on such fundamental types. Thus, from the twelfth century onwards, the dead are described in ecclesiastical documents as marching in hordes like a terrifying, invincible army (*exercitus mortuorum*). While some characters disappeared, Harlequin became the dead's most popular leader, so that the Wild Hunt was widely known as *Mesnie Hellequin* or *Familia Herlechini*.

HARLEQUIN

On the Sunday of Shrovetide, 1981, Carnival masquerades are in full swing in Moena, a village of the Ladin ethnic minority in the Dolomites (northern Italy) most popular among skiers and mountaineers. The main cortège of maskers moves slowly down the main village street towards the central square. It is led by two *Arlechign*, the local variant of the Harlequin-type masks which are found all over the Alps. The maskers wear a chequered costume in bright, contrasting colours, a tall, pointed cap, heavy leather boots and harness bells. Their faces are disguised by a loose veil that gives them an eerie, featureless and ghostly appearance (fig. 135). The Harlequins carry horse whips which they swing in ominous, searching motions at the crowd of urchins cheeringly accompanying the masquerade. Suddenly, as they approach the crowd of tourists and villagers waiting in the square, the Harlequins charge into the swarm of youngsters, delivering merciless blows with their whips. There is total confusion. From a picturesque and nostalgic village festival, the event has reverted to the more traditional pattern of performance involving ribaldry, transgression and carnivalesque violence. The Ladins have turned from the carriers of a bygone, charming cultural heritage into the 'peasants' and 'savages' that they are now accused of being by the outraged onlookers.

These episodes, chosen from many possible historical and contemporary examples, synthesise crucial aspects of European masking practices. A thin but steady thread links together, across space and time, the masks, the living and the dead, witches and dream-like experiences, ritual violence, the illness induced by malevolent spirits and the cure provided by courageous young men. Why then are certain themes in European masquerading apparently so resilient? Why is it that, although nineteenth-century folklorists lamented the impending demise of time-honoured masking practices, their late twentieth-century colleagues can still describe them as fully functioning? How are we to interpret the persistence of characters such as Harlequin in their demon-like form, despite the changes he underwent in becoming an exclusively comic mask?

Masks: mastering transformation in times of crisis

In Europe, as elsewhere, masks are paradoxical in their use: as Mesnil and Napier have noted, they at once transform and fix identities. In concealing individual identity, they simultaneously transform it into something radically different – to the extent that tearing the mask from somebody's face is an act of abomination. Yet at the same time they create 'fixed types', giving definite form to otherwise imprecise symbolic and dramatic characters. In this sense masks simplify mutable individual mood and status by providing permanent identities. They allow a structured, predictable (and therefore repeatable) dramatic narrative to unfold in recurrent events. The role-playing that a masker takes on in choosing this or that masquerading costume, is no simple celebration of freedom and creativity, but formalises action: the behaviour of masks is expected, even prescribed. Thus, we cannot understand masks without considering the action context of the masquerade. Only when a performance is in full swing can the effect of the combination of transformation and fixity be appreciated.

Throughout Europe, masks are often organised in sets of sharply contrasting characters. In several towns of the Basque countries, the 'good'

137. A *Zamalzain* of the Red Masquerade in the Basque countries.

138. *Roitschäggäta* mask, from Wiler in Lötschental (Canton Wallis, Switzerland).

139. (*opposite*) A *Schöni Chläus* (Pretty Chläus) of Urnäsch (Canton Appenzell, Switzerland). See fig. 134.

mascarade rouge ('red masquerade') is opposed to the 'bad' *mascarade noire* ('black masquerade'). The contrast is between elegant and well-behaved characters such as the *Zamalzain* (a variation on the pan-European character of the Hobby Horse) (figs 136 and 137), and repulsive, obscene and transgressive masks such as the *Caldereros* (tinkers). In the same area, at Ituren, the masked cortège features the colourful, jolly *Yoaldunak* as against the dull and beastly *Artza* (bear) and its following of Wild Men-type characters. In Lötschental (Switzerland), the monstrous and aggressive *Tschäggäta* masks (fig. 138) find a gentle, attractive counterpart in the *Otschi* masks, while in Urnäsch the elegant *Schöni Chläus* (Pretty Chläus) are opposed to the monstrous *Wüescht Chläus* (Ugly Chläus) (figs 134, 139). An opposition between the *Schöneperchten* and the *Schiachtperchten* (Handsome and Ugly Perchten) is to be found in a variety of types across the southern German cultural area, from the Bodensee across to the Tyrol, the area of Salzburg and Upper Carinthia with links to Slovenia, where masks of the *Pehtra*-type are widespread (figs 140 and 141). More generally, in the Tyrolean Fasnacht, a marked opposition polarises the *Wilder* and the *Schleicher* mask-types (figs 142, 143).

If in the German region the contrast is between idealised human characters and negative, monstrous animal types, in the Neo-Latin cultural area the contrast is often between opposite extremes of human types. In Friul (northeastern Italy) the opposition is between *Bielinis* and *Brutinis* (Handsome and Ugly), the same contrast as is found among mask types in the Dolomites (figs 144, 145), and in the Carnivals of Schignano, Bagolino and Pontecaffaro in Lombardy. Such oppositions are not only aesthetic. Ugly masks behave transgressively, and often aggressively. Their counterparts, instead, go to extremes of gentleness and affectation in balancing their opposites' behaviour.

The mask-type of the Fool, central to so many masked performances throughout Europe, constitutes the ambiguous and paradoxical synthesis of these oppositions. Handelman's recent cross-cultural analysis of the function and symbolism of ritual Fools describes the character as oscillating between extremes and straddling irreconcilable opposites. In his rhymed tirades against the moral fickleness of his fellow villagers, the *Bufon* of the Val di Fassa proclaims the paradox that has fascinated generations of writers, thinkers and masqueraders: 'If you think I am a fool/then you have got to be a bigger fool than me!' (fig. 146). At once attractive and repulsive, witty and dumb, elegant and clumsy, the Fool swings back and forth between the extremes represented in other masks. For this reason, he incarnates an (albeit unreasonable) synthesis: the impossibility of existing at once as one thing and its opposite without, literally, 'going mad'.

In the sense outlined above, masks embody an outlook that polarises the alternative ways of being in the world. They schematise character types

140. *Schöneperchten* masks (Austria).

141. *Schiachtperchten* in Bischofshofen (Austria) on the Sunday following 6 January.

143. *Schleicher* masks in Telfs (Austria).

142. (*opposite*) *Wilder* masks in Telfs (Austria).

and behaviour by going all the way in opposite directions. The commonly held view of masks as avatars of unbridled, 'transgressive' creativity, applies perhaps to their manifestations in contemporary urban contexts. In the tightly structured masquerades of European popular culture, though, such qualities are often brought to the fore only to be revoked, so to speak, by opposite forms of behaviour. Set in the middle, ambiguous and uneasy, the Fool is the morality player of the insanity of extremes. In masking, everything is possible not so much because 'anything goes', but rather because extremes are predictable and their combination is folly.

But why, then, extremes? Why monsters, hobby horses, horns, bears, Wild Men, with their improbably handsome and attractive counterparts? Masks perform in Europe, as elsewhere, at critical junctures in the yearly cycle. The seasonal passages (the end of the harvest, the beginning of a new agricultural cycle, the transition from winter to spring) variously intertwined with elements of a more 'arbitrary', historical and cultural nature (Christmas, Carnival and Lent, Whitsuntide) are the occasions for masquerading. Like all transitions, these times are critical. Life is no longer what it was and not yet what it will become. A vacuum opens, and there

144. Two *Méscres a Bel* (Handsome Masks) in the 1980 Carnival of Campitello (Val di Fassa, Dolomites).

is a danger of regression or of a half-baked transformation that would compromise renewal, survival and growth.

Passing seasons, returning dead and nasty young men

Several years ago Claude Lévi-Strauss analysed the structural relation that cross-culturally links children to the ancestors. If the cyclical movement of life is represented in the alternation of the seasons, then the human cycle of life and death translates into the succession of generations. At the moment that the old year dies and the new is born, the cosmos is held in a balance. The dead come into close contact with the new generation. A relation between children and the dead ancestors is thus established. Like all transitions, this is also a point of crisis: the two worlds are better kept

145. A couple of *Méscres a Burt* (Ugly Masks) in the same Carnival.

146. The *Bufon* (Fool) harassing the audience during the 1980 Carnival in Penia (Dolomites, Italy).

rus uoit empressées,
de nouueaux appas,
fond de uos pensées,
le haut, pour le bas.

separated lest chaos ensue. Something must be done to re-establish and confirm a regulatory boundary.

In Italy, Spain and other areas of southern Europe, on the Eve of Halloween (All Souls) the dining room was readied with a proper reception for the returning dead. A sacrificial gift (a feast) was given away in exchange for the dead happily returning to their abodes underground, from where they would enable the growth of the crops in the forthcoming season. Elsewhere in Europe, and especially in Britain, the same effect was achieved by similar means. Here the children acted as the representatives of the ancestors. They went around disguised as frightening monsters or witches, occasionally carrying skull-like masks and collecting offerings: the choice was to give and live, or refuse and die. Giving to the children meant settling the score with the ancestors, honouring and satisfying them and sending them safely back to their realm.

Halloween was the date of the Celtic New Year. It was Christianised in the Middle Ages by the powerful Gallic Church, perhaps under the influence of Irish missionaries, to become the Feast of All Saints and All Souls. Halloween was also the date when the last products of the new harvest (late at northern latitudes) were brought in, and thanks were given to those supernatural forces which had helped in bringing it about. The chief mediators between the gods of vegetation and the living were the ancestors, according to a pattern that cross-culturally associates growth, death and fertility. The calendrical association between masks and the dead does not stop here, however. Medieval documents certify that masked dances involving the Hobby Horse – a mask-type diffused all over Europe – were conducted in cemeteries on Saints' days in *ludi* (games, plays) which were relentlessly, but ineffectually, attacked by the Church authorities. Who were involved in such *ludi*?

In medieval rural communities there was a strong correlation between young men, masquerading and the dead. At certain crucial times in the yearly cycle, the village youths had the mandatory right/duty to stage masked pageants. Across northern Russia, during the Christmas season, the young bachelors of the rural communities used to mask as dead people. A mock funeral was performed. One of the youths was laid in a coffin and carried from house to house, where the young maidens kissed the 'dead man' amid lewd jokes and obscenities. In the last century, a priest of the district of Vel'sk (a division of Vologda) complained that his parishioners

147. *A ce moulin chacun sa femme amène pour les remoudre* (Everybody brings his wife to this mill to have her remoulded). Anonymous etching on copper, France, c.1660. 23 x 23 cm. The motif of the rejuvenation of women is widespread in European folklore. Carnivals in South Tyrol and the Dolomites still feature 'The Old Women's Mill' as one of the key performances. The motif articulates issues pertaining to fertility and renewal, the passage from Winter to Spring, the initiation of young men and – in general – the topsy-turvy world dramatised by the masks.

148. The *Combat of Carnival and Lent*, Peter Brueghel, 1559. Carnival and
Lent are structurally opposed periods within European popular culture.
This opposition constitutes one of the commonest sources of inspiration
for masquerading all over the continent. Often, a masked character
impersonating the excesses of Carnival is tried and sentenced to death by
a 'judge' masked as Lent at the end of *Mardi Gras*.

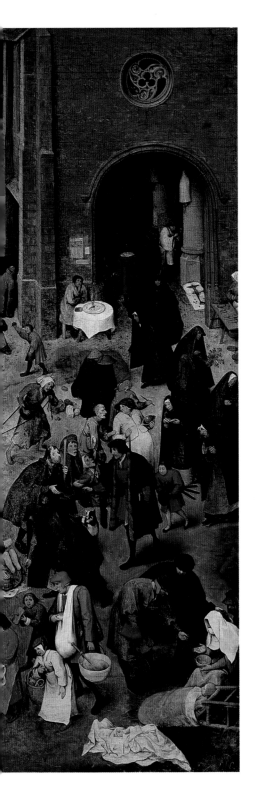

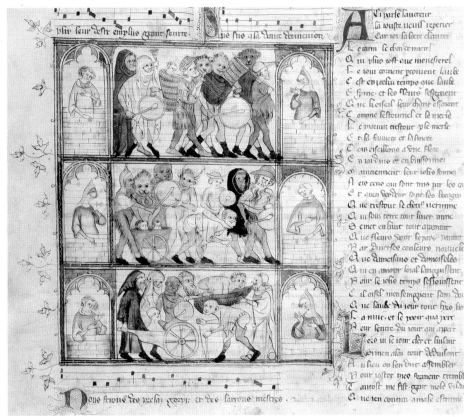

had disinterred a real corpse in order to carry out such a *Mavruch* masquerade. As today, the Twelve Nights between Christmas and Epiphany (that is to say the period set symmetrically across the New Year) were, together with Carnival, the time when masquerades were most numerous and spectacular.

From the Middle Ages up to the eighteenth century and beyond, formalised youth associations such as the Bachelleries and Abbayes de Jeunesse in France and the Società dei Matti in Italy, performed masquerades on behalf of the community. These happened chiefly at Carnival time. In the major urban centres youth masquerading societies were formal, institutionalised groups with statutes and dues, often under the protection of high-powered personalities or professional guilds who would guarantee their immunity in times of trouble. Elsewhere, in rural and mountainous areas of Europe, they were, and often still are, more informally organised. In parts of northern Italy young men, especially the unmarried and those about to be called up to national service (the *coscric* – conscripts), play leading roles in masquerades. Among the German-speaking Mocheni, their association with the souls of the departed is stressed during the Christmas season when they figure prominently in processions that sing the story of the Magi from house to house, collecting alms for requiem masses on behalf of the dead. A high degree of complexity was also reached by the Festas dos Rapazes, celebrated in northeastern Portugal immediately after Christmas to initiate the new generation into adulthood. A widespread dramatic pattern of 'initiation' masquerades involves the performances of mock weddings, ploughing, sowing and other agricultural operations all related to the symbolism of renewal suggested by the masks.

The young bachelors of the community, chiefly those celebrating entry into adulthood, are transitional characters. No longer children, they are not yet fully adult: for instance, they may not yet have the right to court women or drink in bars along with the other men, and neither are they allowed to set up a family of their own. They are the privileged carriers of masks all over Europe. In keeping with their transitional nature, their garb often combines elements of both male and female folk costumes. Across the Alpine region, from the Tyrol to Switzerland, their facial disguises are distinctively asexual, in sharp contrast with the strong sexual connotations of all the other masks.

Let us then take stock of the connections and associations that have been highlighted so far. The dead, the newborn, the forthcoming generation, the death of the old year, the birth of a new season: masking in Europe occurs at certain crucial junctures of the seasonal cycle, New Year being particularly important. Masking involves certain categories of performers to the exclusion of others. In Europe, as elsewhere in the world (with some notable exceptions), women do not perform masquerade. This fact has

been interpreted as a way of reinforcing women's 'symbolical presence' in Carnival's often overtly gender-related symbolism by means of their 'absence'. Among men it is the unmarried youths who have the privilege and duty of performing masks.

To sum up: masquerading establishes correspondences between what Van Gennep has termed 'the cosmic passages' of the seasonal cycle and 'the sociological passages' of human generations. It is as if the transformation of personal identity inherent in the act of masking went alongside the opposite process – the making of transitional, and therefore uncertain and problematic, identities into new, better-focused and therefore safer ones.

The price to be paid: sacrifice, wild men and monsters

Yet, at some time, somebody has to give in order to receive. At the zenith of Carnival, the most significant of European masking events, ritual unfolds along the most dramatic lines of all – the killing of a victim, animal or human.

In Rome the main events of the Carnival were the *agoni di Testaccio*, a series of prize races involving different classes of participants, both on foot and mounted. The *agoni* of antiquity are the historical antecedents of the modern Carnival. One of the central events of the *agoni di Testaccio* was the hunt of the bear, the bull and the cock, performed in the presence of the Pope. By the thirteenth century the Carnival hunts were given a Christian meaning. However, in Rome, well into the nineteenth century, criminals were executed on the last day of Carnival (*Martedi Grasso*, *Mardi Gras* or Shrove Tuesday) and before the final masquerade of the year. If they were available, Jewish convicts would be put to death on that day. During Carnival, the Jews of Rome were made the target of insult and abuse by a frenzied crowd during a special foot race organised for them as part of the *agoni*. The Jewish community was also made the financial scapegoat of the feast. Its leader was forced to hand over a large sum of money to enable the Roman Senate to sponsor the Carnival (the practice was abolished in 1848 by Pius IX).

If the singling out of a sacrificial victim to end the time for masquerading achieved its dramatic climax in Rome, this was only the most disturbing of a set of similar practices which accompanied the performance of masks all over Europe.

Until its abolition in the 1960s, the role of scapegoat was sustained in several towns of southern Spain by *La Mahoma*, a gigantic head of the Prophet that was exploded at the end of a mock battle between Christians and Moors. The *Keyenoba* Carnival masquerade of Georgia also featured the dramatised deadly contest between the Georgian King and the invading *Keyen*, a ritualised memory of historical events in the region. In Castel Tesino, not far from the Dolomites, the core of Carnival celebrations is a

151. (*overleaf*) The *Gilles* of Binche (Belgium) represent an instance of the 'invention' of popular tradition in recent times.

masquerade that re-enacts the hunt, trial and execution of Biagio delle Castellare, a feudal lord of the fourteenth century infamous in popular memory for his corruption and abuses.

In these events the ritual drama refers to some perception of the conflicts involved in actual historical events. However, such dramatic patterns occur within a framework of other contradictions. Thus throughout the whole European cultural area, Carnival and Lent dovetail into one another, and their contrast becomes a source of ritual symbolism: the period of abundance and excess represented by Carnival fights against that of abstinence, fast and penance represented by Lent. In Spain, France, Italy and Russia, however, the sacrificial victim ritually put to death at the end of Carnival can be a masked character impersonating Carnival itself. In some cases the structure of the ritual drama is elaborated into a full narrative sequence. Before execution, Carnival's will is read out. It may turn out to be a grotesque and spicy commentary about the social life of the community in the past year: a list of 'sins' that Carnival is about to expiate on everyone's behalf. Several different characters may be substituted for the embodiment of Carnival. Across the Alps, a Wild Man-type mask is hunted out and killed, as happens to the *Om* and *Femena dal Bosk* of Bormio, in Lombardy, or to the *Salvanel* and his wife *Cavra Barbana* in the Val di Fiemme, Dolomites.

Wild Men-types blend into the limitless variations of the bear-, and ultimately 'monster'-type masks that figure in a staggering variety of forms across all of Europe. Arguably the 'Hunt of the Bear' pattern of masquerading is the most widespread narrative structure of European masquerades, from the Pyrenees to Romania. The hunt may be conducted by the young men of the village, and thus become part of the display of prowess and skill that accompanies their initiation into adulthood. Also, the Bear is itself a symbol of the forthcoming spring. In the French cultural area especially, 2 February is the date when the bear is thought to come out of hibernation and test the weather for signs of spring. 'To hunt the Bear out' can thus be a metaphor for human intervention in the seasonal transition, and 'to put the Bear to death' a redemptive sacrificial gesture. Before the masked figure of the Bear – and its dramatic equivalents – is finally harnessed and ritually put to death, it might be allowed to roam wild in villages, causing havoc, stealing and molesting women, as with the *Tschäggata* of Lötschental in Switzerland or the *Salvanel* in the Val di Fiemme.

Structures and history

On 10 December 1520, shortly after Luther had publicly burnt the Papal Bull condemning his doctrines, a group of students staged a grotesque Carnival procession to poke fun at the Papacy. This happened before what Weidkhun has described as the 'structural incompatibility' between Prot-

152. The *Surovaskari* of the Pernik region, on 13 January, St Basil's Day.

estantism and Carnival had wiped away many masking traditions from Protestant Europe. Elsewhere, however, the changes promoted by the cultural dynamics of the Renaissance kept on their set course. On 13 February 1850, shortly after the bloody end of the 1848 revolution, a puppet was paraded in the streets of Vidauban, near St Tropez in what was for most onlookers the yearly execution of the Carnival scapegoat. In fact, the masquerade had been staged by well-known left-wingers, and the town authorities interpreted the old symbolism as a reference to the period of *La Terreur*: the organisers of the masquerade were arrested and tried.

These episodes epitomise the historical destiny of the relationship between the structure and the content of European masquerades. With the

accelerating pace of social and economic change, the symbolic references embodied in the old mythological complexes are shifted to the issues of the day. In the contemporary Carnivals of Nice, Binche (Belgium) (fig. 151), Venice and Viareggio (fig. 153), the masquerades may retain elements drawn from popular culture. However, this is more a consequence of the self-conscious formalisation of 'folklore' as a genre of nationalist cultural policy in the nineteenth century than a matter of organic continuity. Today masquerading is more involved with the celebration and enhancement of national culture and communal pride – of local, ethnic or minority identity – than with appeasing the dead or promoting a new generation to adulthood. Scholars have analysed such issues in the developments of the Romantic period, in the current re-invention of tradition in many European contexts, and in the metropolitan situations which gave birth to new forms of masquerading such as those seen at the Notting Hill Carnival in London and on the American continent.

We began by explaining the basic power of a mask as being that of a mechanism for ordering the world, a capacity at once to transform and yet to fix identity. From such an ambiguous process masks derive the historical endurance to withstand the shift of their symbolic references and to come through to the present day in still recognisable form: as Descartes wrote, *larvatus prodeo* ('I advance masked').

153. *Fiat Voluntas Tua* (Thy Will be Done). A Carnival float in Viareggio (Italy) satirises Gianni Agnelli, the Italian car tycoon.

BIBLIOGRAPHY

Introduction/General

ADAMS, M. J. 1981. Interpretations of masking in Black Africa ritual. *Africa-Tervuren*, 27.2, pp. 46–51.

BIEBUYCK, DANIEL. 1973. *Lega Culture: art initiation and moral philosophy among a Central African people*, University of California Press.

BINKLEY, A. 1987. Avatar of Power: southern Kuba masquerade figures in a funerary context. *Africa* 57:1, pp. 75–97.

BOURGEOIS, ARTHUR P. 1984. *Art of the Yaka and Suku*, Alain et Françoise Chattin.

GOONATILLEKA, M. H. 1978. *Masks and mask systems of Sri Lanka*. Colombia.

GREGOR, JOSEPH. 1937. *Masks of the world*. New York, London [reissued 1968].

KAPFERER, BRUCE. 1983. *A celebration of demons, exorcism and the aesthetics of healing in Sri Lanka*. Bloomington.

LEACH, R. 1989/90. Masquerade – the presentation of self in holi-day life. *Cambridge Anthropology* 13:3, pp. 47–69.

LOMMEL, ANDREAS. 1972. *Masks: their meaning and function*, London [German original published 1970].

LOVICONI, ALAIN. 1981. *Masks and Exorcisms of Sri Lanka*. Editions Errance.

NAPIER, DAVID. 1986. *Masks, Tranformation and Paradox*. University of California Press.

ROBERTS, A. F. 1990. Tabwa masks: an old hat trick of the human race. *African Arts*, 23:2, pp. 36–47.

TURNER, VICTOR. 1967. *The Forest of Symbols, Aspects of Ndembu ritual*. Cornell University Press.

VANSINA, JAN. 1978. *The Children of Woot, a history of the Kuba peoples*. University of Wisconsin Press.

WHISTLER, LAURENCE. 1947. *The English Festivals*. William Heinemann Ltd.

African Masking

BIEBUYCK, D. 1973. *Lega Culture*, University of California Press.

BINKLEY, DAVID. 1987. Avatar of Power: Southern Kuba masquerade figures in a funerary context. *Africa*, 57, 1, pp. 75–97.

BRAIN, R. and POLLOCK, A. 1971. *Bangwa Funerary Sculpture*, Duckworth.

BRAVMANN, R. 1974. *Islam and Tribal Art*, Cambridge University Press.

CLARKE, J. DESMOND. 1953. Dancing Masks From Somaliland. *Man*, no. 72, pp. 49–51.

DREWAL, H. J. and DREWAL M.T. 1983. *Gelede: Art and Female Power Among the Yoruba*, Indiana University Press.

GLAZE, ANITA. 1981. *Art and Death in a Senufo village*, Indiana University Press.

HORTON, ROBIN. 1960. *Gods as Guests*, Nigeria Magazine, Lagos.
1963. The Kalabari 'Ekine' Society. *Africa*, 33, pp. 94–114.
1963. *Kalabari Sculpture*. Department of Antiquities, Nigeria.

JEDREJ, C. 1974. An Analytical Note on the Land and Spirits of the Sewa Mende. *Africa*, 44, pp. 38–45.

1980. A comparison of some masks from North America, Africa, and Oceania. *Journal of Anthropological Research*, pp. 220–9.
1986. Dan and Mende masks: a structural comparison. *Africa*, pp. 71–9.

JONES, G. I. 1984. *The Art of Eastern Nigeria*, Cambridge University Press.

KAFIR, SIDNEY L. (ed.). 1988. *West African Masks and Cultural Systems*, Musée Royal de l'Afrique Centrale, Tervuren, Ann. vol. 126.

KUBIK, GERHARD. 1969. Masks of the Mbwela. *Geographica*, Revisita da Sociedade de Geografia de Lisboa, 20.

MOORE, F. 1738. *Travels into the Inland Parts of Africa*. Printed for the author by Edward Cave.

MUYAGA, GANGAMBI. 1974–5. *Les Masques Pende*, 2 vols, Ceeba Publications, Bandundu.

OTTENBERG, SIMON. 1975. *Masked Rituals of Afikpo*, University of Washington Press.

PICTON, JOHN. 1974. Masks and the Igbirra. *African Arts*, VII, 2, pp. 38–41.
1988. Some Ebira reflexions on the energies of women. *African Languages and Cultures*, 1, 1, pp. 61–76.
1990. What's in a mask? *African Languages and Cultures*, III, 2.

DE SOUSBERGHE, L. 1958. *L'Art Pende*, Académie Royale de Belgique, Tome IX, fasc. 2.

TONKIN, ELIZABETH. 1979. Masks and Power. *Man*, 14, 2, pp. 237–48.

TURNER, VICTOR. 1967. *The Forest of Symbols*, Cornell University Press.

VANSINA, JAN. 1955. Initiation Rituals of the Bushong. *Africa*, 25, pp. 138–53.

WHITE, C. M. N. 1953. Notes on the Circumcision Rites of the Balovale Tribes. *African Studies*, 12, pp. 41–56.

YOSHIDA, KENJI. 1992. Masks and Transformation among the Chewa of Eastern Zambia. *Senri Ethnological Studies*, No. 31, pp. 203–73.

Masks in Oceania

BODROGI, TIBOR. 1961. *Art in North-East New Guinea*. Budapest.

BOULAY, ROGER. 1990. *De jade et de nacre: patrimoine artistique kanak*. Paris.

CLUNIE, FERGUS and LIGAIRI, WALESI. 1983. Traditional Fijian spirit masks and spirit masquers. *Domodomo Fiji Museum Quarterly*, June 1983:1, pp. 46–71.

CODRINGTON, R. H. 1891. *The Melanesians*. Oxford [reprinted 1972, New York].

CORBIN, GEORGE A. 1979. The Art of the Baining: New Britain. *Exploring the visual art of Oceania*, S. M. Mead (ed.), Honolulu, pp. 159–79.
1982. Chachet Baining art. *Expedition*, 24:2, pp. 5–16.
1984. The Central Baining revisited. *Res*, 7/8, pp. 44–69.
1990. Salvage art history among the Sulka of Wide Bay, East New Britain, Papua New Guinea. *Art and identity in Oceania*, A. Hanson and L. Hanson (eds), Bathurst, pp. 67–83.

CRAWFORD, ANTHONY L. 1975. *Gogodala: Lagoon dwellers of the Gulf*, Land and People Series no. 3. Port Moresby.
1981. *Aida: Life and ceremony of the Gogodala*. Bathurst.

DARK, PHILIP. 1974. *Kilenge art and life*. London.

DAVENPORT, WILLIAM. 1964. Sculpture from La Grande Terre. *Expedition*, Fall 1964, pp. 1–19.

ERRINGTON, FREDERICK KARL. 1974. *Karavar: masks and power in a Melanesian ritual*. Ithaca, London.

FELDMAN, JEROME and RUBINSTEIN, DONALD H. 1986. *The Art of Micronesia*. Honolulu.

FRASER, DOUGLAS FERRAR. 1978. *Torres Straits sculpture*. New York, London.

GELL, ALFRED. 1975. *Metamorphosis of the cassowaries: Umeda society, language and ritual*. London School of Economics Monographs on Social Anthropology no. 51. London.

GERBRANDS, ADRIAN A. (ed.). 1967. *The Asmat of New Guinea: the journal of Michael Clark Rockefeller*. New York.

HADDON, A. C. (ed.). 1901–35. *Reports of the Cambridge Anthropological Expedition to the Torres Strait*, 6 vols. Cambridge.

HELFRICH, KLAUS. 1973. *Malanggan 1: Bildwerke von Neuirland*. Berlin.

HESSE, KARL and AERTS, THEO. 1982. *Baining life and lore*. Port Moresby.

HIDIKATA, HISAKATSO. 1973. Stone images of Palau. *Guam College Micronesian Area Research Center Publication*, no. 3.

HILL, ROWENA. 1982. *Fieldtrip to the Sulka area of Wide Bay, East New Britain; to collect and document the masks used at an ordination ceremony, January 1982*. (Unpublished report for the National Museum and Art Gallery, Port Moresby.)

KAEPPLER, ADRIENNE L. 1963. Ceremonial masks: a Melanesian art style. *Journal of the Polynesian Society*, 72, pp. 118–38.

KING, JAMES. 1785. *A Voyage to the Pacific Ocean . . .* 2nd ed., vol. 3. London.

KONRAD, GUNTER et al. 1981. *Asmat: Leben mit den Ahnen*. Glasshütten/Ts.

KOOIJMAN, SIMON. 1984. *Art, art objects and ritual in the Mimika culture*. Mededelingen van het Rijksmuseum voor Volkenkunde Leiden, no. 24. Leiden.

KRAUSE, F. 1906. Zur Ethnologie der Inseln Nissan. *Jahrbuch der Stadt. Museum für Völkerkunde zu Leipzig*, 1, pp. 44–159.

LEWIS, PHILLIP H. 1973. Changing memorial ceremonial in northern New Ireland. *Journal of the Polynesian Society*, 82, pp. 141–53.

LINCOLN, LOUISE et al. 1987. *Assemblage of spirits: idea and image in New Ireland*. New York.

LOSCHE, DIANE. 1982. *The Abelam: a people of Papua New Guinea*. Sydney.

McKESSON, JOHN A. 1990. In search of the origins of the New Caledonian mask. *Art and identity in Oceania*, A. Hanson and L. Hanson (eds), Bathurst, pp. 84–92.

MAMIYA, CHRISTIAN J. and SUMNIK, EUGENIA C. 1982. *Hevehe: art, economics and status in the Papuan Gulf*. Museum of Cultural History, UCLA Monograph Series no. 18. Los Angeles.

MOORE, DAVID R. 1984. *The Torres Strait collections of A. C. Haddon: a descriptive catalogue*. London.
1989. *Arts and crafts of Torres Strait*. Princes Risborough.

NEWTON, DOUGLAS. 1961. *Art styles of the Papuan Gulf*. New York.

1971. *Crocodile and cassowary: religious art of the upper Sepik River, New Guinea*. New York.

PARKINSON, R. 1907. *Dreissig Jahre in der Südsee*. Stuttgart.

POWELL, WILFRED. 1884. *Wanderings in a wild country; or, three years amongst the cannibals of New Britain*. London.

ROSE, ROGER G. 1990. The Masked Tamate of Vanikoro. *Art and identity in Oceania*, A. Hanson and L. Hanson (eds), Bathurst, pp. 111–28.

SARASIN, FRITZ. 1929. *Atlas zur Ethnologie der Neu-Caledonier und Loyalty-Insulaner*. Munich.

SMIDT, DIRK. 1990. Symbolic meaning in Kominimung masks. *Sepik heritage: tradition and change in Papua New Guinea*, Nancy Lutkehaus et al. (eds), Durham, North Carolina, pp. 509–22.

SPEISER, FELIX. 1990. *Ethnology of Vanuatu: an early twentieth century study*. Bathurst [German original published 1923].

TEILHET, JEHANNE H. 1979. The equivocal nature of masking tradition in Polynesia. *Exploring the visual art of Oceania*, S. M. Mead (ed.), Honolulu, pp. 192–201.

WARDWALL, ALLEN. 1971. *The Art of the Sepik River*. Chicago.

WILLIAMS, F. E. 1924. *The Natives of the Purari Delta*. Territory of Papua Anthropology Report no. 5, Port Moresby.
1940. *Drama of Orokolo: the social and ceremonial life of the Elema*. Oxford [reprinted 1969].

ZELENETZ, MARTIN and GRANT, JILL. 1980. Kilenge Narogo: ceremonies, resources and prestige in a West New Britain society. *Oceania*, 51:2, pp. 98–117.

Fictions and Parodies: Masquerade in Mexico and Highland South America

BORUEGI, S. F. 1955. Pottery Mask Traditions in Mesoamerica. *Southwestern Journal of Anthropology*, 11, pp. 205–13.

CASO, A. et al. 1945. *Máscaras Mexicanas*. Mexico D. F. Sociedad de Arte Moderno.

CRUMRINE, N. ROSS and HALPIN, M. (eds). 1983. *The Power of Symbols, Masks and Masquerade in the Americas*. Vancouver.

ESSER, J. BRODY (ed.). 1988. *Behind the Mask in Mexico*. Santa Fe.

GUERRA GUTIERREZ, A. (n.d.). *El Carnaval de Oruro a Su Alcance*. Oruro.

KLEIN, C. 1986. Masking Empire: The material effects of masks in Aztec Mexico. *Art History*, 9, 2, pp. 135–67.

Musées Royaux d'Art et d'Histoire. 1982. *Máscaras de México*. Brussels.

MURATORIO, R. 1981. *A Feast of Corpus Christi: Dance costumes from Ecuador from the Olga Fisch Collection*. Washington.

SHELTON, A. 1988. Realm of the Fire Serpent. *British Museum Society Bulletin*, 55, pp. 20–5.

WARMAN, A. 1972. *La Danza de Moros y Cristianos*. Mexico.

Masks from the Northwest Coast of America

BOAS, FRANZ. 1897. The Social Organisation and Secret Societies of the Kwakiutl Indians. *Report of the US National Museum for 1895*, pp. 311–738.
1955. *Primitive Art*. Dover, New York.

HAWTHORN, AUDREY. 1979. *Kwakiutl Art*. University of Washington Press, Seattle.

HOLM, BILL. 1972. *Crooked Beak of Heaven: Masks and Other Ceremonial Art of the Northwest Coast*. Seattle.
1983. *Smoky-Top: The Art and Times of Willie Seaweed*. Seattle.

1983. *The Box of Daylight: Northwest Coast Indian Art.* Seattle.

JONAITIS, ALDONA, (ed.). 1991. *Chiefly Feasts. The Enduring Kwakiutl Potlatch.* London and Seattle.

DE LAGUNA, FREDERICA. 1972. *Under Mount St. Elias: The History and Culture of the Yakutat Tlingit.* Smithsonian Contributions to Anthropology 7.

RITZENTHALER, ROBERT and LEE A. PARSONS (eds). 1966. *Masks of the Northwest Coast: the Samuel A. Barrett Collection.* Milwaukee.

SUTTLES, WAYNE, (ed.). 1990. Northwest Coast. Vol. 7 of *Handbook of North American Indians.* Washington DC.

Japanese Masks: Ritual and drama

BERNEGGER, BRIGIT. 1993. *Nō Masken im Museum Rietburg, Zurich.* Zurich.

INOURA and KAWATAKE. 1981. *The Traditional Theatre of Japan.* New York and Tōkyō.

KEENE, DONALD. 1966. *Nō, The Classical Theatre of Japan.* Tōkyō.

MARUOKA and YOSHIKOSHI. 1969. *Nō.* Ōsaka.

NAKANISHI and KOMMA. 1983. *Nō Masks.* Ōsaka.

1967. Nō/Kyōgen Men. *Nihon no Bijutsu* no. 108. Tōkyō.

NISHIWAKA, KYŌTARŌ. 1978. *Bugaku Masks.* Tōkyō.

NOGAMI, TOYOICHIRŌ. 1938. *Nō Masks.* Tōkyō.

NOMA, SEIROKU. 1957. *Arts and Crafts of Japan* no. 1, 'Masks'. Vermont and Tōkyō.

1981. *Komen no bi – shūkyō to geinō.* Special exhibition catalogue, Kyōto National Museum. Kyōto.

1990. *The Hōryūji Treasures.* Tōkyō.

YOSHIKOSHI and HATA. 1982. *Kyōgen.* Ōsaka.

Face Value: The mask in Greece and Rome

BIEBER, M. 1961. *The History of the Greek and Roman Theater.* Princeton.

BROOKE, I. 1962. *Costume in Greek Classic Drama.* London.

PICKARD-CAMBRIDGE, A. 1988. *The Dramatic Festivals of Athens,* second ed. revised by J. Gould and D. M. Lewis, Oxford.

SIMON, E. 1982. *The Ancient Theatre.* London.

WILES, D. 1991. *The Masks of Menander.* Cambridge.

Masks in Ancient Egypt: The image of divinity

BONNET, HANS. 1952. *Reallexikon der Ägyptischen Religionsgeschichte,* pp. 440–2. Berlin.

D'AURIA, SUE, LACOVARA, PETER and ROEHRIG, CATHARINE H. 1988. *Mummies & Magic. The Funerary Arts of Ancient Egypt.* Boston.

EDGAR, C. C. 1905. *Catalogue Général des Antiquités Égyptiennes du Musée du Caire, Nos. 33101–33285: Graeco-Egyptian Coffins, Masks and Portraits.* Cairo.

GEORGE, BEATE. 1981. 'Geheimer Kopf' – 'Kopf aus Lapislazuli'. Altägyptische Tradition und Mumienmasken römischer Zeit. *Medelhavsmuseet Bulletin,* 16, pp. 15–38.

GUIMET, E. 1912. *Les Portraits d'Antinoë au Musée Guimet.* Paris.

GRIMM, GÜNTER. 1974. *Die Römischen Mumienmasken aus Ägypten.* Wiesbaden.

KÁKOSY, LÁSZLÓ. 1980. Eine Frauenmaske im Medelhavsmuseet. *Medelhavsmuseet Bulletin,* 15, pp. 16–24.

MURRAY, M. A. 1934. Ritual Masking. *Mélanges Maspero* I, pp. 251–5 & plate.

ROOT, MARGARET COOL. 1979. *Faces of Immortality. Egyptian Mummy Masks, Painted Portraits, and Canopic Jars in the Kelsey Museum of Archaeology.* University of Michigan.

SEEBER, CHRISTINE. 1980. Maske. *Lexikon der Ägyptologie* 3, cols. 1196–9.

SWEENEY, DEBORAH. 1993. Egyptian Masks in Motion, *Göttinger Miszellen* 135, pp. 101–4.

WILDUNG, DIETRICH. 1990. Geheimnisvolle Gesichter. *Antike Welt* 4, pp. 206–21.

WOLINSKI, ARELENE. 1986. Ancient Egyptian Ceremonial Masks. *Discussions in Egyptology,* 6, pp. 47–53.

The Other Within: Masks and masquerades in Europe

AGULHON, M. 1970. *La République au Village.* Paris.

BENDIX, R. 1985. *Progress and Nostalgia: Silvesterklausen in Urnäsch, Switzerland.* Berkeley.

BLOCH, M. and PARRY, J. (eds). 1982. *Death and the Regeneration of Life.* Cambridge.

BOISSEVAIN, J. (ed.). 1992. *Revitalising European Rituals.* London.

BOITEUX, M. 1976. Les juifs dans le Carnaval de la Rome Moderne (XVe–XVIIIe Siècles). *Mélanges de l'École Française de Rome. Moyen Age – Temps Modernes,* 88, pp. 745–87.

CARO BAROJA, J. 1965. *El Carnaval: Analisis Historico-Cultural.* Madrid.

CARRASCO, M. S. 1976. Christians and Moors in Spain: History, Religion, Theatre. *Cultures* 1, pp. 87–116.

CHAMBERS, E. K. 1903. *The Mediaeval Stage,* 2 vols. Oxford.

CHIABÒ, M. and DOGLIO, F. (eds). 1989. *Il Carnevale dalla Tradizione Arcaica alla Traduzione Colta del Rinascimento.* Rome.

CHIBNALL, M. (ed.). 1969–80. *The Ecclesiastical History of Orderic Vitalis,* 6 vols. Oxford.

CLEMENTI, F. 1938–9. *Il Carnevale Romano nelle Cronache Contemporanee,* 2 vols. Città di Castello.

COHEN, A. 1980. Drama and Politics in the Development of a London Carnival. *Man,* 1, pp. 65–87.

DA MATTA, R. 1981. *Carnavals, Malandros e Heróis.* Rio de Janeiro.

DÖRRER, A. 1949. *Tiroler Fasnacht: Innerhalb der Alpenländischen Winter – und Vorfrühlingsbräuche.* Vienna.

GINZBURG, C. 1981. Charivari, Associations Juvéniles, Chasse Sauvage. *Le Charivari,* J. Le Goff and J.-C. Schmitt (eds), Paris, pp. 131–40.

1983. *The Night Battles: Witchcraft and Agrarian Cults in the Sixteenth and Seventeenth Centuries.* London.

1989. *Ecstasies: Deciphering the Witches' Sabbath.* New York.

GRINBERG, M. and KINSER, S. 1983. Les Combats de Carnaval et de Carême – Trajets d'un Métaphore. *Annales,* 1, pp. 65–98.

HALE, C. 1976. *A Dictionary of British Folk-Customs.* London.

HANDELMAN, D. 1981. The Ritual Clown: Attributes and Affinities. *Anthropos,* 76, pp. 321–70.

HEERS, J. 1983. *Fêtes des Fous et Carnavals.* Paris.

HILL, E. 1972. *The Trinidad Carnival: Mandate for a National Theatre.* Austin.

HUNTINGTON, R. and METCALF, P. 1979. *Celebrations of Death – The Anthropology of Mortuary Ritual.* Cambridge.

KAPFHAMMER, G. (ed.). 1977. *Brauchtum in den Alpenländern.* Munich.

KINSER, S. 1990. *Carnival, American Style: Mardi Gras at New Orleans and Mobile.* London.

KLIGMAN, G. 1977. *Calus: Symbolic Transformation in Romanian Ritual*. Chicago.

KURET, N. 1984. *Maske Slovenskih Pokrajin*. Ljubljani.

LE GOFF, J. and SCHMITT, J.-C. (eds). 1981. *Le Charivari*. Paris.

LÉVI-STRAUSS, C. 1952. Le Père Noël Supplicié. *Les Temps Modernes*, 77.

LEYDI, R. and PIANTA, B. (eds). 1976. *Brescia e il Suo Territorio*. Milan.

LEYDI, R. and SANGA, G. (eds). 1978. *Como e il Suo Territorio*. Milan.

LONGA, G. 1912. *Usi e Costumi del Bormiese*. Sondrio.

MESNIL, M. 1976. The Masked Festival: Disguise or Affirmation?. *Cultures*, 2, pp. 11–29.

MEULI, K. 1943. *Schweizer Masken*. Zurich.

MURARO, L. 1976. *La Signora del Gioco*. Milan.

NAPIER, D. 1984. *Masks, Transformation and Paradox*. Berkeley.
1967. *New Catholic Encyclopedia*. New York.

NICOLOSO CICERI, A. 1982. *Tradizioni Popolari in Friuli*, 2 vols. Reana del Rojale.

PEREIRA, B. 1973. *Máscaras Portuguesas*. Lisbon.

PFAUNDLER, W. 1981. *Fasnacht in Tirol: Telfer Schleicherlaufen*. Wörgl.

POLA-FALLETTI DI VILLAFALLETTO, G. C. 1932–45. *Associazioni Giovanili e Feste Antiche – Loro Origini*, 3 vols. Milan.

POPPI, C. 1986. Il Tipo Simbolico 'Uomo Selvaggio': Motivi, Funzioni e Ideologia. *Mondo Ladino*, X, 95–118.
1988. Il Bello, il Brutto e il Cattivo: Elementi d'Analisi Simbolica ed Estetica delle Maschere della Val di Fassa. *Faceres:*

Maschere Lignee del Carnevale di Fassa, F. Chiocchetti (ed.), Vigo di Fassa/Vich, pp. 7–52.

PRATI, A. 1905. *Folklore Trentino*. Venice.

PROPP, V. JA. 1978. *Feste Agrarie Russe – Una Ricerca Storico-Etnografica*. Bari.

RUKHADZE, J. and CHITAYA, G. 1976. Festivals and Traditions in the Georgian Soviet Socialist Republic. *Cultures*, 2, pp. 70–81.

SCHMIDT, L. 1971. *Perchtenmasken in Österreich*. Vienna.

SCHMITT, J.-C. 1988. *Religione, Folklore e Societa'nell'Occidente Medievale*. Bari.

SCRIBNER, B. 1978. Reformation, Carnival and the World Turned Upside-Down. *Social History*, 3, pp. 303–29.

SECCO, G. 1989. *Viva, Viva Carnevale!* Belluno.

SIDRO, A. (ed.). *Le Carnaval, la Fête et la Communication*. Nice.

TOSCHI, P. 1976. *Le Origini del Teatro Italiano*. Turin.

VALLERANT, J. 1974–5. Réflexions à Propos de la Collection de Masques du Lötschental du Musée d'Ethnographie de Genève. *Bulletin Annuel, Musée d'Ethnographie*, pp. 15–63.

VAN GENNEP, A. 1947. *Manuel de Folklore Français Contemporain*, 2 vols. Paris.

VON ZIMBURG. n.d. *Der Perchtenlauf in der Gastein*. Vienna.

WESSELOFSKY. 1988. Alichino e Aredodesa. *Giornale Storico della Litteratura Italiana*, XII, pp. 325–43.

WEIDKUHN, P. 1976. Carnival in Basel: Playing History in Reverse. *Cultures*, 1, pp. 29–53.

ZAMON DAVIES, N. 1975. *Society and Culture in Early Modern France*. London.

ZINTZO-GARMENDIA, B. and TRUFFAUT, T. 1988. *Carnavals Basques*. Toulouse.

ILLUSTRATION ACKNOWLEDGEMENTS

Abbreviation: BM = Photo by courtesy of the Trustees of the British Museum.

PREFACE
BM Add. 23921.

INTRODUCTION: ABOUT FACE
1. BM 1886.12-7.9.
2. BM 1902.6-24.1.
3. BM 1927-112.
4. BM 1944.Oc.2.943. Presented by Mrs H. G. Beasley, 1944.
5. BM 1926.Am.10.
6. BM 1562. Christy Collection.
7. BM 1941.Am.1.1. Collected by George T. Emmons. Beasley Collection.
8. BM 1945.10-17.506.
9. BM OA +7108.
10. BM Cat. of bronzes 877.
11. BM 29476.
12. BM 29474.

AFRICAN MASKING
13. BM 1904.11-22.1.
14. BM 1938.6-8.80.
15. BM 1957.Af.12.3.
16. BM 1993.Af.9.30.
17. BM 1905.6-9.2.
18. BM 1951.Af.34.1.
19. BM 1954.Af.23.492.
20. BM 1981.Af.7.1.
21. BM 1954.Af.23.Q.
22. BM 1955.Af.3.2.
23. BM 1956.Af.27.299.
24. BM 1910.4-20.473.
25. BM 1910.4-20.478.
26. BM 1956.Af.27.14.
27. BM 1956.Af.27.2.
28. BM 1956.Af.27.40.
29. BM 1909.118.

MASKS IN OCEANIA
30. BM 1884.7-28.25. Presented by the Duke of Bedford, 1884.
31. BM 1889.2-8.13. Presented by Capt. Charles Cross RN.
32. BM 1954.Oc.6.260. Presented by the Trustees of the Wellcome Historical Medical Museum.
33. BM 1855.12-20.169. From the Museum of Haslar Hospital, presented by the Lords of the Admiralty, 1855.
34. BM +2491. Presented by A. W. Franks, 1885.
35. BM +2489. Presented by A. W. Franks, 1885.
36. BM +2486. Presented by A. W. Franks, 1885.
37. BM 1929.3-4.12. Presented by the Lord Leverhulme, 1929.
38. BM 1975.Oc.1.1. Presented by the British Museum Society.
39. BM 1930.5-10.3.
40. BM 1987.Oc.5.11. Collected by Noel McGuigan, 1987.
41. BM 1936.7-20.70. Presented by Lord Moyne. BM 1919.7-18.1. BM 1979.Oc.4.1.
42. BM 1983.Oc.9.1. BM +5882. Acquired from the Ethnographic Museum, Munich, 1892.
43. BM 1884.7-28.19. Presented by the Duke of Bedford, 1884.
44. BM 1986.Oc.3.1.
45. BM 1982.Oc.9.1.
46. BM 1944.Oc.2.1818. Presented by Mrs H. G. Beasley, 1944.
47. BM 1983.Oc.12.3. Collected by Rowena Hill.
48. BM TAH 78. Presented by Capt. James Cook.

FICTIONS AND PARODIES:
MEXICO AND HIGHLAND SOUTH AMERICA
49. Mario Carrieri.
50. Arnold Nelson/Omniquests.
51. Linden Museum, Stuttgart.
52. BM 1910.12-25.
53. BM 1949 6-295
54. Robert and Lisa Sainsbury Collection, University of East Anglia, Norwich.
55. Mario Carrieri.
56. Oriana Badelay.
57. The University Museum, University of Pennsylvania.
58. BM 1956.Am.X6.
59. BM ST 401.
60. BM ST 400.
61. BM Q87.Am.3.
62. Oriana Badelay.
63. BM 1985.Am.32.54, 55.
64. BM 1938.10-21.450, 451, 452, 453, 454, 455.
65. BM 1981.Am.6.17, 22, 23, 24, 40, 55.
66. Anthony Shelton Collection, Royal Pavilion Art Gallery and Museums, Brighton.
67. Royal Pavilion Art Gallery and Museums, Brighton.
68. Anthony Shelton.

MASKS FROM THE NORTHWEST COAST OF AMERICA
69. BM 1986.Am.18.1. Collected in Hawaii before 1830.
70. BM 1896.12.0.2. Christy Fund. Presented by Sir A. W. Franks.
71. BM 1850.6-3.2. Presented by a Lieutenant Hall, R.N.
72. BM 1939.Am.11.3.
73. BM 1944.Am.2.135. Presented by Mrs H. G. Beasley.
74. BM 1954.W.Am.5. 1169. Presented by the Trustees of the Wellcome Historical Medical Museum.
75. BM +252. Presented to the Christy Collection by Sir A. W. Franks, 1877.
76. BM 1944.Am.2. 192 and 195. Presented by Mrs H. G. Beasley.
77. BM +217. Presented to the Christy Collection by Fleetwood Sandeman, 1877.
78. BM 7184. Presented to the Christy Collection by Henry J. Gardiner, 1871.
79. BM +436. Collected at Fort Rupert, British Columbia, before 1875. Presented by Sir A. W. Franks to the Christy Collection.
80. BM 1944.Am.2.133. Collected in the 1860s. Presented by Mrs H. G. Beasley.
81. BM 6437. Presented to the Christy Collection by J. L. Brenchley, 1870.
82. BM 4928. Presented to the Christy Collection by Frederick Whymper.
83. BM +221. Presented to the Christy Collection by Fleetwood Sandeman, 1877.
84. BM 1981.Am.12.18. Presented by the Trustees of the Wellcome Historical Medical Museum.
85. BM 1944.Am.2.193. Presented by Mrs H. G. Beasley.
86. BM 1924.7-8.1.

JAPANESE MASKS: RITUAL AND DRAMA
87. BM 1985.7-16.1.
88. BM 1954.10-21.1.
89. BM 1978.4-2.2.
90. BM JP 296.
91. Toyoko Takahashi.
92. BM 1945.10-17.401.
93. BM OA 7197.
94. BM 1986.11-3.2.

95. BM OA 7111.
96. (and front jacket). BM 1946.12-16.2.
97. BM 1957.11-20.1.
98. BM.
99. Courtesy of G. Irvine, photo BM Photo Service.

FACE VALUE: THE MASK IN GREECE AND ROME
100. BM Cat. of vases E180.
101. Historisches Museum der Stadt, Vienna.
102. Staatliche Antikensammlungen, Munich/ Studio Koppermann.
103. Museo Archeologico Nazionale, Naples.
104. BM Cat. of vases B210.
105. BM Cat. of vases F151.
106. Staatliche Museen zu Berlin – Preussicher Kulturbesitz.
107. Museo Archeologico Nazionale, Naples.
108. BM Cat. of sculpture 2440.
109. BM Cat. of terracottas C520.
110. BM Cat. of sculpture 1767.
111. BM Cat. of terracottas C81.
112. BM Cat. of sculpture 2450.
113. BM 1989.1-30.1.
114. BM Cat. of Roman sarcophagi 25.
115. BM Cat. of gems 2205.
116. Palazzo dei Conservatori, Rome.

MASKS IN ANCIENT EGYPT:
THE IMAGE OF DIVINITY
117. BM 22912.
118. BM 46631.
119. BM 29770.
120. BM 48001.
121. BM 6679.
122. BM 20745.
123. BM 50668.
124. BM 49376.
125. BM 30845.
126. BM 29477.
127. BM 22109.
128. BM 63841.
129. BM 24781.
130. BM 24780.
131. BM 24902.
132. BM 55304.
133. BM 30723.

THE OTHER WITHIN: MASKS AND MASQUERADES IN EUROPE
134. Photo SNTO.
135. Istitut Cultural Ladin, Vich/Vigo di Fassa.
136. Collections/Brian Shuel.
137. Musée International du Carnaval et du Masque, Binche, Belgium.
138. Photo SNTO.
139. Photo SNTO.
140. Musée International du Carnaval et du Masque, Binche, Belgium. Photo M. Revelard.
141. K. Kitamura.
142. Alex Orloff.
143. K. Kitamura.
144. Istitut Cultural Ladin, Vich/Vigo di Fassa.
145. Istitut Cultural Ladin, Vich/Vigo di Fassa.
146. Istitut Cultural Ladin, Vich/Vigo di Fassa.
147. Bibliothèque National, Paris.
148. Kunsthistorisches Museum, Vienna, inv. GG 1016.
149. Bibliothèque National, Paris.
150. J. M. Steinlein.
151. Alex Orloff.
152. J. M. Steinlein.
153. Alex Orloff.

INDEX